www.EffortlessMath.com

... So Much More Online!

✓ FREE Math lessons

✓ More Math learning books!

✓ Mathematics Worksheets

✓ Online Math Tutors

Need a PDF version of this book?

Please visit www.EffortlessMath.com

Algebra II Exercise Book:

Student Workbook

By

Reza Nazari

& Ava Ross

All inquiries should be addressed to:

info@effortlessMath.com

www.EffortlessMath.com

ISBN-13: 978-1-970036-84-8

ISBN-10: 1-970036-84-2

Published by: Effortless Math Inc

www.EffortlessMath.com

Description

This Algebra workbook's new edition has been updated to replicate questions appearing on the most recent Algebra II test. Here is intensive preparation for the Algebra II course, and a precious learning tool for Algebra takers who need extra practice in math to raise their Algebra II scores. After completing this workbook, you will have solid foundation and adequate practice that is necessary to ace the Algebra II Test. **This workbook is your ticket to score higher on Algebra II test.**

The updated version of this hands-on workbook represents extensive exercises, math problems, sample Algebra II questions, and quizzes with answers and detailed solutions to help you hone your math skills, overcome your exam anxiety, and boost your confidence -- and do your best to defeat Algebra II exam on test day.

Each of math exercises is answered in the book which will help you find your weak areas and raise your scores. This is a unique and perfect practice book to beat the Algebra II Test.

Separate math chapters offer a complete review of the Algebra course, including:

- Equations and Inequalities
- Quadratic Functions and System of Equations
- Polynomial Operations
- Functions and their applications
- Imaginary Numbers
- Matrices and Matrix Equations
- Exponential and Logarithmic Functions
- Trigonometric Functions
- ... and many more Algebra II topics

The surest way to succeed on Algebra II is with intensive practice in every math topic tested-- and that's what you will get in *Algebra II Exercise Book*. Each chapter of this focused format has a comprehensive review created by Math experts that goes into detail to cover all of the content likely to appear on the Algebra II test.

Effortless Math Workbook for the Algebra II contains many exciting and unique features to help you improve your Algebra scores, including:

- Content 100% aligned with the Algebra II courses
- Written by experienced Math tutors and test experts
- Complete coverage of all Algebra II concepts and topics which you will be tested
- Over 2,500 additional Algebra II math practice questions in both multiple-choice and grid-in formats with answers grouped by topic, so you can focus on your weak areas
- Abundant Math skill building exercises to help you approach different question types that might be unfamiliar to you

- Exercises on different Algebra II topics such as equations, polynomials, exponents and radicals, functions, etc.

This Algebra II Workbook and other Effortless Math Education books are used by thousands of students each year to help them review core content areas, brush-up in math, discover their strengths and weaknesses, and achieve their best scores on the Algebra test.

Get ready for the Algebra II Test with a PERFECT Workbook!

About the Author

Reza Nazari is the author of more than 100 Math learning books including:

– **Math and Critical Thinking Challenges:** For the Middle and High School Student
– **GED Math in 30 Days**
– **ASVAB Math Workbook 2018 - 2019**
– **Effortless Math Education Workbooks**
– **and many more Mathematics books …**

Reza is also an experienced Math instructor and a test–prep expert who has been tutoring students since 2008. Reza is the founder of Effortless Math Education, a tutoring company that has helped many students raise their standardized test scores—and attend the colleges of their dreams. Reza provides an individualized custom learning plan and the personalized attention that makes a difference in how students view math.

To ask questions about Math, you can contact Reza via email at:
reza@EffortlessMath.com

Find Reza's professional profile at:
goo.gl/zoC9rJ

Contents

Chapter 1: Fundamentals and Building Blocks

Topics that you'll learn in this chapter:

- ✓ The Order of Operation
- ✓ Scientific Notation
- ✓ Exponents Operations
- ✓ Evaluating Expressions
- ✓ Simplifying Algebraic Expressions

Order of Operations

✍ *Evaluate each expression.*

1) $5 + (4 \times 2) =$

2) $13 - (2 \times 5) =$

3) $(16 \times 2) + 18 =$

4) $(12 - 5) - (4 \times 3) =$

5) $25 + (14 \div 2) =$

6) $(18 \times 5) \div 5 =$

7) $(48 \div 2) \times (-4) =$

8) $(7 \times 5) + (25 - 12) =$

9) $64 + (3 \times 2) + 8 =$

10) $(20 \times 5) \div (4 + 1) =$

11) $(-9) + (12 \times 6) + 15 =$

12) $(7 \times 8) - (56 \div 4) =$

13) $(4 \times 8 \div 2) - (17 + 11) =$

14) $(18 + 8 - 15) \times 5 - 3 =$

15) $(25 - 12 + 45) \times (95 \div 5) =$

16) $28 + \left(15 - (32 \div 2)\right) =$

17) $(6 + 7 - 4 - 9) + (18 \div 2) =$

18) $(95 - 17) + (10 - 25 + 9) =$

19) $(18 \times 2) + (15 \times 5) - 12 =$

20) $12 + 8 - (42 \times 4) + 50 =$

Scientific Notation

✏️ **Write each number in scientific notation.**

1) $0.113 =$

2) $0.02 =$

3) $2.5 =$

4) $20 =$

5) $60 =$

6) $0.004 =$

7) $78 =$

8) $1,600 =$

9) $1,450 =$

10) $91,000 =$

11) $2,000,000 =$

12) $0.0000006 =$

13) $354,000 =$

14) $0.000325 =$

15) $0.00023 =$

16) $56,000,000 =$

17) $21,000 =$

18) $78,000,000 =$

19) $0.0000022 =$

20) $0.00012 =$

✏️ **Write each number in standard notation.**

21) $3 \times 10^{-1} =$

22) $5 \times 10^{-2} =$

23) $1.2 \times 10^{3} =$

24) $2 \times 10^{-4} =$

25) $1.5 \times 10^{-2} =$

26) $4 \times 10^{3} =$

27) $9 \times 10^{5} =$

28) $1.12 \times 10^{4} =$

29) $3 \times 10^{-5} =$

30) $8.3 \times 10^{-5} =$

Exponents Operations

✍ **Simplify.**

1) $(4^2)^2 =$

2) $(6^2)^3 =$

3) $(2 \times 2^3)^4 =$

4) $(4 \times 4^4)^2 =$

5) $(3^3 \times 3^2)^3 =$

6) $(5^4 \times 5^5)^2 =$

7) $(2 \times 2^4)^2 =$

8) $(2^6)^2 =$

9) $(11x^5)^2 =$

10) $(4x^2y^4)^4 =$

11) $(2x^4y^4)^3 =$

12) $(3x^2y^2)^2 =$

13) $(3x^4y^3)^4 =$

14) $(2x^6y^8)^2 =$

15) $(12x^3x)^3 =$

16) $(2x^9x^6)^3 =$

17) $(5x^{10}y^3)^3 =$

18) $(4x^3x^3)^2 =$

19) $(3x^3.5x)^2 =$

20) $(10x^{11}y^3)^2 =$

21) $(9x^7y^5)^2 =$

22) $(4x^4y^6)^5 =$

23) $(3x.4y^3)^2 =$

24) $\left(\frac{5x}{x^2}\right)^2 =$

25) $\left(\frac{x^4y^4}{x^2y^2}\right)^3 =$

26) $\left(\frac{25x}{5x^6}\right)^2 =$

27) $\left(\frac{x^8}{x^6y^2}\right)^2 =$

28) $\left(\frac{xy^2}{x^3y^3}\right)^{-2} =$

29) $\left(\frac{2xy^4}{x^3}\right)^2 =$

30) $\left(\frac{xy^4}{5xy^2}\right)^{-3} =$

Evaluating Expressions

 Evaluate each expression using the values given.

1) $2x + 4y$,

   $x = 3, y = 2$

2) $8x + 5y$,

   $x = 1, y = 5$

3) $-2a + 4b$,

   $a = 6, b = 3$

4) $4x + 7 - 2y$,

   $x = 7, y = 6$

5) $5z + 12 - 4k$,

   $z = 5, k = 2$

6) $2(-x - 2y)$,

   $x = 6, y = 9$

7) $18a + 2b$,

   $a = 2, b = 8$

8) $4x \div 3y$,

   $x = 3, y = 2$

9) $2x + 15 + 4y$,

   $x = -2, y = 4$

10) $4a - (15 - b)$,

   $a = 4, b = 6$

11) $5z + 19 + 8k$,

   $z = -5, k = 4$

12) $xy + 12 + 5x$,

   $x = 7, y = 2$

13) $2x + 4y - 3 + 2$,

   $x = 5, y = 3$

14) $\left(-\frac{12}{x}\right) + 1 + 5y$,

   $x = 6, y = 8$

15) $(-4)(-2a - 2b)$,

   $a = 5, b = 3$

16) $10 + 3x + 7 - 2y$,

   $x = 7, y = 6$

17) $9x + 2 - 4y + 5$,

   $x = 7, y = 5$

18) $6 + 3(-2x - 3y)$,

   $x = 9, y = 7$

19) $2x + 14 + 4y$,

   $x = 6, y = 8$

20) $4a - (5a - b) + 5$,

   $a = 4, b = 6$

Simplifying Algebraic Expressions

✍ *Simplify each expression.*

1) $3(x + 9) =$

2) $(-6)(8x - 4) =$

3) $7x + 3 - 3x =$

4) $-2 - x^2 - 6x^2 =$

5) $3 + 10x^2 + 2 =$

6) $8x^2 + 6x + 7x^2 =$

7) $5x^2 - 12x^2 + 8x =$

8) $2x^2 - 2x - x =$

9) $4x + 6(2 - 5x) =$

10) $10x + 8(10x - 6) =$

11) $9(-2x - 6) - 5 =$

12) $2x^2 + (-8x) =$

13) $x - 3 + 5 - 3x =$

14) $2 - 3x + 12 - 2x =$

15) $32x - 4 + 23 + 2x =$

16) $(-6)(8x - 4) + 10x =$

17) $14x - 5(5 - 8x) =$

18) $23x + 4(9x + 3) + 12 =$

19) $3(-7x + 5) + 20x =$

20) $12x - 3x(x + 9) =$

21) $7x + 5x(3 - 3x) =$

22) $5x(-8x + 12) + 14x =$

23) $40x + 12 + 2x^2 =$

24) $5x(x - 3) - 10 =$

25) $8x - 7 + 8x + 2x^2 =$

26) $2x^2 - 5x - 7x =$

27) $7x - 3x^2 - 5x^2 - 3 =$

28) $4 + x^2 - 6x^2 - 12x =$

29) $12x + 8x^2 + 2x + 20 =$

30) $2x^2 + 6x + 3x^2 =$

31) $23 + 15x^2 + 8x - 4x^2 =$

32) $8x - 12x - x^2 + 13 =$

Answers of Worksheets – Chapter 1

The Order of Operation

1) 13
2) 3
3) 50
4) −5
5) 32
6) 18
7) −96

8) 48
9) 78
10) 20
11) 78
12) 42
13) −12
14) 52

15) 1,102
16) 27
17) 9
18) 72
19) 99
20) −98

Scientific Notation

1) 2×10^{-2}
2) 2.5×10^0
3) 2×10^1
4) 6×10^1
5) 4×10^{-3}
6) 7.8×10^1
7) 1.6×10^3
8) 1.45×10^3
9) 9.1×10^4
10) 2×10^6

11) 6×10^{-7}
12) 3.54×10^5
13) 3.25×10^{-4}
14) 2.3×10^{-4}
15) 5.6×10^7
16) 2.1×10^4
17) 7.8×10^7
18) 2.2×10^{-6}
19) 1.2×10^{-4}
20) 0.3

21) 0.05
22) 1,200
23) 0.0002
24) 0.015
25) 4,000
26) 900,000
27) 11,200
28) 0.00003
29) 0.000083

Exponents Operations

1) 4^4
2) 6^6
3) 2^{16}
4) 4^{10}
5) 3^{15}
6) 5^{18}
7) 2^{10}
8) 2^{12}
9) $121x^{10}$
10) $256x^8y^{16}$
11) $8x^{12}y^{12}$

12) $9x^4y^4$
13) $81x^{16}y^{12}$
14) $4x^{12}y^{16}$
15) $1,728x^{12}$
16) $8x^{45}$
17) $125x^{30}y^9$
18) $16x^{12}$
19) $225x^8$
20) $100x^{22}y^6$
21) $81x^{14}y^{10}$
22) $1,024x^{20}y^{30}$

23) $144x^2y^6$
24) $\frac{25}{x^2}$
25) x^2y^2
26) $\frac{25y^4}{x^{10}}$
27) $\frac{x^4}{y^4}$
28) x^4y^2
29) $\frac{4y^8}{x^4}$
30) $\frac{125}{y^6}$

Evaluating Expressions

1) 14
2) 33
3) 0
4) 23
5) 29
6) −48
7) 52

8) 2
9) 27
10) 7
11) 26
12) 61
13) 21
14) 39

15) 64
16) 26
17) 50
18) −111
19) 58
20) 7

Simplifying Algebraic Expressions

1) $3x + 27$
2) $-48x + 24$
3) $4x + 3$
4) $-7x^2 - 2$
5) $10x^2 + 5$
6) $15x^2 + 6x$
7) $-7x^2 + 8x$
8) $2x^2 - 3x$
9) $-24x + 12$
10) $90x - 48$
11) $-18x - 59$
12) $2x^2 - 8x$
13) $-2x + 2$
14) $-5x + 14$
15) $34x + 19$

16) $-38x + 24$
17) $54x - 25$
18) $59x + 24$
19) $-x + 15$
20) $-3x^2 - 15x$
21) $-15x^2 + 22x$
22) $-40x^2 + 74x$
23) $2x^2 + 40x + 12$
24) $5x^2 - 15x - 10$
25) $2x^2 + 16x - 7$
26) $2x^2 - 12x$
27) $-8x^2 + 7x - 3$
28) $-5x^2 - 12x + 4$
29) $8x^2 + 14x + 20$
30) $5x^2 + 6x$
31) $11x^2 + 8x + 23$
32) $-x^2 - 4x + 13$

Chapter 2: Equations and Inequalities

Topics that you'll learn in this chapter:

- ✓ One–Step Equations
- ✓ Multi–Step Equations
- ✓ Graphing Single–Variable Inequalities
- ✓ One–Step Inequalities
- ✓ Multi-Step Inequalities

One–Step Equations

✍ *Solve each equation.*

1) $2x = 20, x =$ ____

2) $4x = 16, x =$ ____

3) $8x = 24, x =$ ____

4) $6x = 30, x =$ ____

5) $x + 5 = 8, x =$ ____

6) $x - 1 = 5, x =$ ____

7) $x - 8 = 3, x =$ ____

8) $x + 6 = 12, x =$ ____

9) $x - 2 = 17, x =$ ____

10) $8 = 12 + x, x =$ ____

11) $x - 5 = 4, x =$ ____

12) $2 - x = -12, x =$ ____

13) $16 = -4 + x, x =$ ____

14) $x - 4 = -25, x =$ ____

15) $x + 12 = -9, x =$ ____

16) $14 = 18 - x, x =$ ____

17) $2 + x = -14, x =$ ____

18) $x - 5 = 15, x =$ ____

19) $25 = x - 5, x =$ ____

20) $x - 3 = -12, x =$ ____

21) $x - 12 = 12, x =$ ____

22) $x - 12 = -25, x =$ ____

23) $x - 13 = 32, x =$ ____

24) $-55 = x - 18, x =$ ____

25) $x - 12 = 18, x =$ ____

26) $20 = 5x, x =$ ____

27) $x - 30 = 20, x =$ ____

28) $x - 12 = 32, x =$ ____

29) $36 - x = 3, x =$ ____

30) $x - 14 = 14, x =$ ____

31) $19 - x = -15, x =$ ____

32) $x - 19 = -35, x =$ ____

Multi–Step Equations

✎ *Solve each equation.*

1) $2x + 3 = 5$

2) $-x + 8 = 5$

3) $3x - 4 = 5$

4) $-(2 - x) = 5$

5) $2x - 18 = 12$

6) $4x - 2 = 6$

7) $2x - 14 = 4$

8) $5x + 10 = 25$

9) $8x + 9 = 25$

10) $-3(2 + x) = 3$

11) $-2(4 + x) = 4$

12) $20 = -(x - 8)$

13) $2(2 - 2x) = 20$

14) $-12 = -(2x + 8)$

15) $5(2 + x) = 5$

16) $2(x - 14) = 4$

17) $-28 = 2x + 12x$

18) $3x + 15 = -x - 5$

19) $2(3 + 2x) = -18$

20) $12 - 2x = -8 - x$

21) $10 - 3x = 14 + x$

22) $10 + 10x = -2 + 4x$

23) $24 = (-4x) - 8 + 8$

24) $12 = 2x - 12 + 6x$

25) $-12 = -4x - 6 + 2x$

26) $4x - 12 = -18 + 5x$

27) $5x - 10 = 2x + 5$

28) $-7 - 3x = 2(3 - 2x)$

29) $x - 2 = -3(6 - 3x)$

30) $10x - 56 = 12x - 114$

31) $4x - 8 = -4(11 + 2x)$

32) $-5x - 14 = 6x + 52$

Graphing Single–Variable Inequalities

 Draw a graph for each inequality.

1) $x > 2$
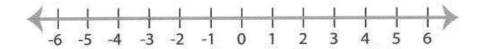

2) $x < 5$
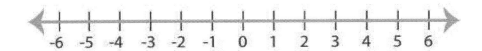

3) $x > -1$
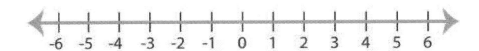

4) $x > 3$
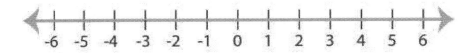

5) $x < -5$

6) $x > -2$
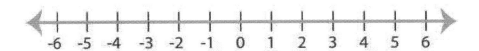

7) $x < 0$
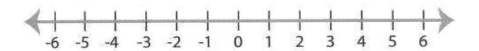

8) $x > 4$
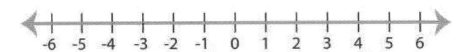

One–Step Inequalities

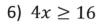 *Solve each inequality and graph it.*

1) $x + 2 \geq 3$

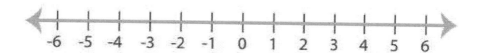

2) $x - 1 \leq 2$

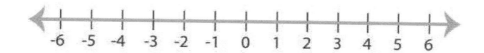

3) $2x \geq 12$

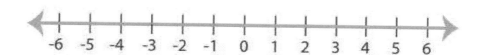

4) $4 + x \leq 5$

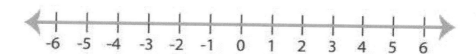

5) $x + 3 \leq -3$

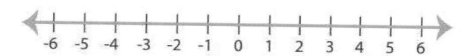

6) $4x \geq 16$

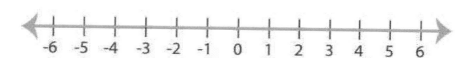

7) $9x \leq 18$

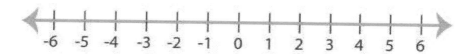

8) $x + 2 \geq 7$

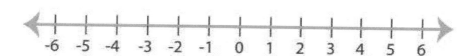

Multi-Step Inequalities

✎ *Solve each inequality.*

1) $x - 2 \leq 6$

2) $3 - x \leq 3$

3) $2x - 4 \leq 8$

4) $3x - 5 \geq 16$

5) $x - 5 \geq 10$

6) $2x - 8 \leq 6$

7) $8x - 2 \leq 14$

8) $-5 + 3x \leq 10$

9) $2(x - 3) \leq 6$

10) $7x - 5 \leq 9$

11) $4x - 21 < 19$

12) $2x - 3 < 21$

13) $17 - 3x \geq -13$

14) $9 + 4x < 21$

15) $3 + 2x \geq 19$

16) $6 + 2x < 32$

17) $4x - 1 < 7$

18) $3(3 - 2x) \geq -15$

19) $-(3 + 4x) < 13$

20) $20 - 8x \geq -28$

21) $-3(x - 7) > 21$

22) $\dfrac{2x + 6}{4} \leq 10$

23) $\dfrac{4x + 8}{2} \leq 12$

24) $\dfrac{3x - 8}{7} > 1$

25) $4 + \dfrac{x}{3} < 7$

26) $\dfrac{9x}{7} - 7 < 2$

27) $\dfrac{4x + 12}{4} > 1$

28) $15 + \dfrac{x}{5} < 12$

Answers of Worksheets – Chapter 2

One–Step Equations

1) 10	12) 14	23) 45
2) 4	13) 20	24) −37
3) 3	14) −21	25) 30
4) 5	15) −21	26) 4
5) 3	16) 4	27) 50
6) 6	17) −16	28) 42
7) 11	18) 20	29) 33
8) 6	19) 30	30) 28
9) 19	20) −9	31) 34
10) −4	21) 24	32) −16
11) 9	22) −13	

Multi–Step Equations

1) 1	12) −12	23) −6
2) 3	13) −4	24) 3
3) 3	14) 2	25) 3
4) 7	15) −1	26) 6
5) 15	16) 16	27) 5
6) 2	17) −2	28) 13
7) 9	18) −5	29) 2
8) 3	19) −6	30) 29
9) 2	20) 20	31) −3
10) −3	21) −1	32) −6
11) −6	22) −2	

Graphing Single–Variable Inequalities

1)

2)

3)

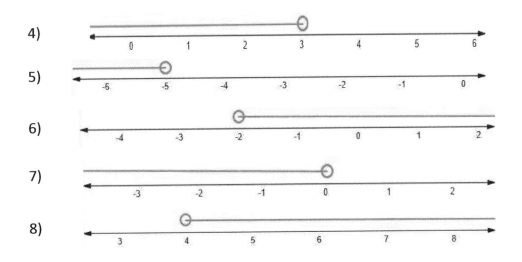

One–Step Inequalities

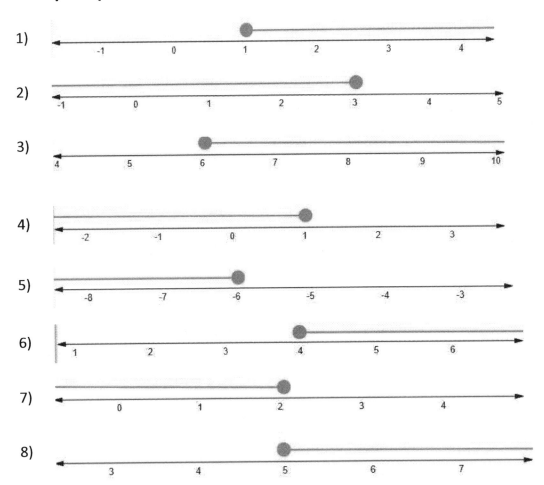

Multi-Step Inequalities

1) $x \leq 8$
2) $x \geq 0$
3) $x \leq 6$
4) $x \geq 7$
5) $x \geq 15$
6) $x \leq 7$
7) $x \leq 2$
8) $x \leq 5$
9) $x \leq 6$
10) $x \leq 2$

11) $x < 10$
12) $x < 12$
13) $x \leq 10$
14) $x < 3$
15) $x \geq 8$
16) $x < 13$
17) $x < 2$
18) $x \leq 4$
19) $x > -4$
20) $x \leq 6$

21) $x < 0$
22) $x \leq 17$
23) $x \leq 4$
24) $x > 5$
25) $x < 9$
26) $x < 7$
27) $x > -2$
28) $x < -15$

Chapter 3: System of Equations and Quadratic

Topics that you'll learn in this chapter:

- ✓ Systems of Equations

- ✓ Systems of Equations Word Problems

- ✓ Systems of 3 Variable Equations

- ✓ Quadratic

- ✓ Solving Quadratic Equations

- ✓ Quadratic Formula and the Discriminant

- ✓ Solve Quadratic Inequalities

- ✓ Graphing Quadratic Functions

Systems of Equations

✎ *Solve each system of equations.*

1) $-2x + 2y = 4$ $x =$ ___

   $-2x + y = 3$ $y =$ ___

2) $-10x + 2y = -6$ $x =$ ___

   $6x - 16y = 48$ $y =$ ___

3) $y = -8$ $x =$ ___

   $16x - 12y = 32$

4) $2y = -6x + 10$ $x =$ ___

   $10x - 8y = -6$ $y =$ ___

5) $10x - 9y = -13$ $x =$ ___

   $-5x + 3y = 11$ $y =$ ___

6) $-3x - 4y = 5$ $x =$ ___

   $x - 2y = 5$ $y =$ ___

7) $5x - 14y = -23$ $x =$ ___

   $-6x + 7y = 8$ $y =$ ___

8) $10x - 14y = -4$ $x =$ ___

   $-10x - 20y = -30$ $y =$ ___

9) $-4x + 12y = 12$ $x =$ ___

   $-14x + 16y = -10$ $y =$ ___

10) $x + 20y = 56$ $x =$ ___

    $x + 15y = 41$ $y =$ ___

11) $6x - 7y = -8$ $x =$ ___

    $-x - 4y = -9$ $y =$ ___

12) $-3x + 2y = -18$ $x =$ ___

    $8x - 2y = 28$ $y =$ ___

13) $-5x + y = -3$ $x =$ ___

    $3x - 8y = 24$ $y =$ ___

14) $3x - 2y = 2$ $x =$ ___

    $5x - 5y = 10$ $y =$ ___

15) $8x + 14y = 4$ $x =$ ___

    $-6x - 7y = -10$ $y =$ ___

16) $10x + 7y = 1$ $x =$ ___

    $-5x - 7y = 24$ $y =$ ___

Systems of Equations Word Problems

✎ *Solve each word problem.*

1) Tickets to a movie cost $5 for adults and $3 for students. A group of friends purchased 18 tickets for $82.00. How many adults ticket did they buy? _____

2) At a store, Eva bought two shirts and five hats for $154.00. Nicole bought three same shirts and four same hats for $168.00. What is the price of each shirt? _____

3) A farmhouse shelters 10 animals, some are pigs, and some are ducks. Altogether there are 36 legs. How many pigs are there? _____

4) A class of 195 students went on a field trip. They took 19 vehicles, some cars and some buses. If each car holds 5 students and each bus hold 25 students, how many buses did they take? _____

5) A theater is selling tickets for a performance. Mr. Smith purchased 8 senior tickets and 5 child tickets for $136 for his friends and family. Mr. Jackson purchased 4 senior tickets and 6 child tickets for $96. What is the price of a senior ticket? $_____

6) The difference of two numbers is 6. Their sum is 14. What is the bigger number? $_____

7) The sum of the digits of a certain two-digit number is 7. Reversing its digits increase the number by 9. What is the number? _____

8) The difference of two numbers is 18. Their sum is 66. What are the numbers? _____

9) The length of a rectangle is 3 meters greater than 2 times the width. The perimeter of rectangle is 30 meters. What is the length of the rectangle?

_____

10) Jim has 44 nickels and dimes totaling $2.95. How many nickels does he have?

_____

Systems of 3 Variable Equations

✍ *Solve each system of equations.*

1) $x = 3y - 3z + 8$ $x = $ ____

   $z = 4x + 5y - 14$ $y = $ ____

   $3y + 2z = 14$ $z = $ ____

2) $6x - 6y = -12$ $x = $ ____

   $2z = -6x - 6y + 18$ $y = $ ____

   $-8x + 10y + 2z = 16$ $z = $ ____

3) $4x - 8z = 40$ $x = $ ____

   $-6x + 2y - 8z = 40$ $y = $ ____

   $-8x + 4y + 6z = -30$ $z = $ ____

4) $2x - 4y + 2z = -12$ $x = $ ____

   $2x + 10z = -24$ $y = $ ____

   $-2x + 12y + 8z = 6$ $z = $ ____

5) $x - y - 2z = -6$ $x = $ ____

   $3x + 2y = -25$ $y = $ ____

   $-4x + y - z = 12$ $z = $ ____

6) $6x - y + 3z = -9$ $x = $ ____

   $5x + 5y - 5z = 20$ $y = $ ____

   $3x - y + 4z = -5$ $z = $ ____

7) $-5x + 3y + 6z = 4$ $x = $ ____

   $-3x + y + 5z = -5$ $y = $ ____

   $-4x + 2y + z = 13$ $z = $ ____

8) $-6x + 5y + 2z = -11$ $x = $ ____

   $-2x + y + 4z = -9$ $y = $ ____

   $4x - 5y + 5z = -4$ $z = $ ____

9) $4x + 4y + z = 24$ $x = $ ____

   $2x - 4y + z = 0$ $y = $ ____

   $5x - 4y - 5z = 12$ $z = $ ____

10) $-10x + 10y + 6z = -46$ $x = $ ____

    $-10x + 6y - 6z = -22$ $y = $ ____

    $-12x + 12z = -24$ $z = $ ____

Quadratic

✍ Multiply.

1) $(x - 2)(x + 4) =$ _____

2) $(x + 1)(x + 6) =$ _____

3) $(x - 4)(x + 2) =$ _____

4) $(x + 5)(x - 3) =$ _____

5) $(x - 6)(x - 2) =$ _____

6) $(2x + 1)(x - 3) =$ _____

7) $(2x - 1)(x + 4) =$ _____

8) $(2x - 3)(x + 4) =$ _____

9) $(3x + 5)(x - 3) =$ _____

10) $(3x + 4)(2x - 2) =$ _____

✍ Factor each expression.

11) $x^2 - 5x + 4 =$ _____

12) $x^2 + 6x + 8 =$ _____

13) $x^2 + x - 12 =$ _____

14) $x^2 - 7x + 10 =$ _____

15) $x^2 - 4x - 12 =$ _____

16) $2x^2 - 3x - 2 =$ _____

17) $2x^2 + 8x + 8 =$ _____

18) $3x^2 - 14x + 5 =$ _____

19) $3x^2 + 4x + 1 =$ _____

20) $4x^2 - 12x + 8 =$ _____

✍ Solve each equation.

21) $(x + 2)(x - 4) = 0$

22) $(x + 5)(x + 8) = 0$

23) $(2x + 4)(x + 3) = 0$

24) $(3x - 9)(2x + 6) = 0$

25) $x^2 - 11x + 19 = -5$

26) $x^2 + 7x + 18 = 8$

27) $x^2 - 10x + 22 = -2$

28) $x^2 + 3x - 12 = 6$

29) $5x^2 - 5x - 10 = 0$

30) $6x^2 - 6x = 36$

Solving Quadratic Equations

✍ *Solve each equation by factoring or using the quadratic formula.*

1) $(x + 2)(x - 7) = 0$

2) $(x + 3)(x + 5) = 0$

3) $(x - 9)(x + 4) = 0$

4) $(x - 7)(x - 5) = 0$

5) $(x + 4)(x + 8) = 0$

6) $(5x + 7)(x + 4) = 0$

7) $(2x + 5)(4x + 3) = 0$

8) $(3x + 4)(x + 2) = 0$

9) $(6x + 3)(2x + 4) = 0$

10) $(9x + 3)(x + 6) = 0$

11) $x^2 = 2x$

12) $x^2 - 6 = x$

13) $2x^2 + 4 = 6x$

14) $-x^2 - 6 = 5x$

15) $x^2 + 8x = 9$

16) $x^2 + 10x = 24$

17) $x^2 + 7x = -10$

18) $x^2 + 12x = -32$

19) $x^2 + 11x = -28$

20) $x^2 + x - 20 = 2x$

21) $x^2 + 8x = -15$

22) $7x^2 - 14x = -7$

23) $10x^2 = 27x - 18$

24) $7x^2 - 6x + 3 = 3$

25) $2x^2 - 14 = -3x$

26) $10x^2 - 26x = -12$

27) $15x^2 + 80 = -80x$

28) $x^2 + 15x = -56$

29) $6x^2 - 18x - 18 = 6$

30) $2x^2 + 6x - 24 = 12$

31) $2x^2 - 22x + 38 = -10$

32) $-4x^2 - 8x - 3 = -3 - 5x^2$

Quadratic Formula and the Discriminant

✏ *Find the value of the discriminant of each quadratic equation.*

1) $x(x - 1) = 0$

2) $x^2 + 2x - 1 = 0$

3) $x^2 + 3x + 5 = 0$

4) $x^2 - x + 4 = 0$

5) $x^2 + x - 2 = 0$

6) $x^2 + 4x - 6 = 0$

7) $x^2 + 5x + 2 = 0$

8) $2x^2 - 2x - 7 = 0$

9) $2x^2 + 3x + 9 = 0$

10) $2x^2 + 5x - 4 = 0$

11) $5x^2 + x - 2 = 0$

12) $-3x^2 - 6x + 2 = 0$

13) $-4x^2 - 4x + 5 = 0$

14) $-2x^2 - x - 1 = 0$

15) $6x^2 - 2x - 3 = 0$

16) $-5x^2 - 3x + 9 = 0$

17) $4x^2 + 5x - 4 = 0$

18) $8x^2 - 9x = 0$

19) $3x^2 - 5x + 1 = 0$

20) $5x^2 + 6x + 4 = 0$

✏ *Find the discriminant of each quadratic equation then state the number of real and imaginary solutions.*

21) $-x^2 - 9 = 6x$

22) $4x^2 = 8x - 4$

23) $-4x^2 - 4x = 6$

24) $8x^2 - 6x + 3 = 5x^2$

25) $-9x^2 = -8x + 8$

26) $9x^2 + 6x + 6 = 5$

27) $9x^2 - 3x - 8 = -10$

28) $-2x^2 - 8x - 14 = -6$

Quadratic Inequalities

✎ *Solve each quadratic inequality.*

1) $x^2 - 1 < 0$

2) $-x^2 - 5x + 6 > 0$

3) $x^2 - 5x - 6 < 0$

4) $x^2 + 4x - 5 > 0$

5) $x^2 - 2x - 3 \geq 0$

6) $x^2 > 5x + 6$

7) $-x^2 - 12x - 11 \leq 0$

8) $x^2 - 2x - 8 \geq 0$

9) $x^2 - 5x - 6 \geq 0$

10) $x^2 + 7x + 10 < 0$

11) $x^2 + 9x + 20 > 0$

12) $x^2 - 8x + 16 > 0$

13) $x^2 - 8x + 12 \leq 0$

14) $x^2 - 11x + 30 \leq 0$

15) $x^2 - 12x + 27 \geq 0$

16) $x^2 - 16x + 64 \geq 0$

17) $x^2 - 36 \leq 0$

18) $x^2 - 13x + 36 \geq 0$

19) $x^2 + 15x + 36 \leq 0$

20) $4x^2 - 6x - 9 > x^2$

21) $5x^2 - 15x + 10 < 0$

22) $3x^2 - 5x \geq 4x^2 + 6$

23) $4x^2 - 12 > 3x^2 + x$

24) $x^2 - 2x \geq x^2 - 6x + 12$

25) $2x^2 + 2x - 8 > x^2$

26) $4x^2 + 20x - 11 < 0$

27) $-9x^2 + 29x - 6 \geq 0$

28) $-8x^2 + 6x - 1 \leq 0$

29) $12x^2 + 10x - 12 > 0$

30) $18x^2 + 23x + 5 \leq 0$

31) $17x^2 + 15x - 2 \geq 0$

32) $3x^2 + 7x \leq 5x^2 + 3x - 6$

Graphing Quadratic Functions

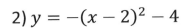 *Sketch the graph of each function. Identify the vertex and axis of symmetry.*

1) $y = 3(x + 1)^2 + 2$

2) $y = -(x - 2)^2 - 4$

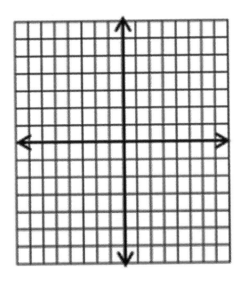

3) $y = 2(x - 3)^2 + 8$

4) $y = x^2 - 8x + 19$

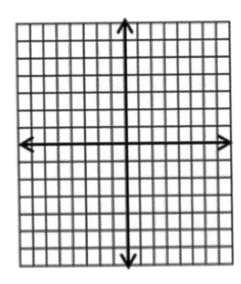

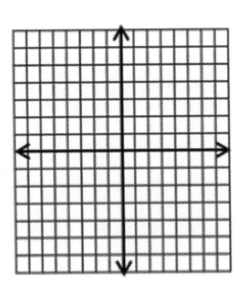

Answers of Worksheets – Chapter 4

Systems of two linear equations

1) $x = -1, y = 1$
2) $x = 0, y = -3$
3) $x = -4$
4) $x = 1, y = 2$
5) $x = -4, y = -3$
6) $x = 1, y = -2$
7) $x = 1, y = 2$
8) $x = 1, y = 1$

9) $x = 3, y = 2$
10) $x = -4, y = 3$
11) $x = 1, y = 2$
12) $x = 2, y = -6$
13) $x = 0, y = -3$
14) $x = -2, y = -4$
15) $x = 4, y = -2$
16) $x = 5, y = -$

Systems of two equations word problems

1) 14
2) $32
3) 8
4) 5
5) $12

6) 10
7) 34
8) $42, 24$
9) 11 *meters*
10) 29

Systems of 3 variable equations

1) $(2, 2, 4)$
2) $(1, 3, -3)$
3) $(0, 0, -5)$
4) $(3, 3, -3)$
5) $(-5, -5, 3)$

6) $(-1, 6, 1)$
7) $(-2, 4, -3)$
8) $(4, 3, -1)$
9) $(4, 2, 0)$
10) $(1, -3, -1)$

Quadratic

1) $x^2 + 2x - 8$
2) $x^2 + 7x + 6$
3) $x^2 - 2x - 8$
4) $x^2 + 2x - 15$
5) $x^2 - 8x + 12$
6) $2x^2 - 5x - 3$
7) $2x^2 + 7x - 4$
8) $2x^2 + 5x - 12$
9) $3x^2 - 4x - 15$
10) $6x^2 + 2x - 8$

11) $(x - 4)(x - 1)$
12) $(x + 4)(x + 2)$
13) $(x - 3)(x + 4)$
14) $(x - 5)(x - 2)$
15) $(x + 2)(x - 6)$
16) $(2x + 1)(x - 2)$
17) $(2x + 4)(x + 2)$
18) $(3x - 1)(x + 5)$
19) $(3x + 1)(x + 1)$
20) $(2x - 2)(2x - 4)$

21) $x = -2, x = 4$
22) $x = -5, x = -8$
23) $x = -2, x = -3$
24) $x = 3, x = -3$
25) $x = 3, x = 8$
26) $x = -2, x = -5$
27) $x = 4, x = 6$
28) $x = 3, x = -6$
29) $x = 2, x = -1$
30) $x = -2, x = 3$

Solving quadratic equations

1) $\{-2, 7\}$
2) $\{-3, -5\}$

3) $\{9, -4\}$
4) $\{7, 5\}$

5) $\{-4, -8\}$
6) $\{-\frac{7}{5}, -4\}$

7) $\{-\frac{5}{2}, -\frac{3}{4}\}$

8) $\{-\frac{4}{3}, -2\}$

9) $\{-\frac{1}{2}, -2\}$

10) $\{-\frac{1}{3}, -6\}$

11) $\{2, 0\}$

12) $\{3, -2\}$

13) $\{2, 1\}$

14) $\{-3, -2\}$

15) $\{1, -9\}$

16) $\{2, -12\}$

17) $\{-2, -5\}$

18) $\{-4, -8\}$

19) $\{-4, -7\}$

20) $\{5, -4\}$

21) $\{-5, -3\}$

22) $\{1\}$

23) $\{\frac{6}{5}, \frac{3}{2}\}$

24) $\{\frac{6}{7}, 0\}$

25) $\{-\frac{7}{2}, 2\}$

26) $\{\frac{3}{5}, 2\}$

27) $\{-\frac{4}{3}, -4\}$

28) $\{-8, -7\}$

29) $\{4, -1\}$

30) $\{3, -6\}$

31) $\{3, 8\}$

32) $\{8, 0\}$

Quadratic formula and the discriminant

1) 1

2) 8

3) −11

4) −15

5) 9

6) 40

7) 17

8) 60

9) −45

10) 57

11) 41

12) 60

13) 96

14) −7

15) 76

16) 189

17) 89

18) 81

19) 13

20) −44

21) 0, *one real solution*

22) 0, *one real solution*

23) −80, *no solution*

24) 0, *one real solution*

25) −224, *no solution*

26) 0, *one real solution*

27) −63, *solution*

28) 0, *one real solution*

Solve quadratic inequalities

1) $-1 < x < 1$

2) $-6 < x < 1$

3) $-1 < x < 6$

4) $x < -5 \text{ or } x > 1$

5) $x \le -1 \text{ or } x \ge 3$

6) $x < -1 \text{ or } x > 6$

7) $x \le -11 \text{ or } x \ge -1$

8) $x \le -2 \text{ or } x \ge 4$

9) $x \le -1 \text{ or } x \ge 6$

10) $-5 < x < -2$

11) $x < -5 \text{ or } x > -4$

12) $x < 4 \text{ or } x > 4$

13) $2 \le x \le 6$

14) $5 \le x \le 6$

15) $x \le 3 \text{ or } x \ge 9$

16) *all real numbers*

17) $-6 \le x \le 6$

18) $x \le 4 \text{ or } x \ge 9$

19) $-12 \le x \le -3$

20) $x < -1 \text{ or } x > 3$

21) $1 < x < 2$

22) $-3 \le x \le -2$

23) $x < -3 \text{ or } x > 4$

24) $x \ge 3$

25) $x < -4 \text{ or } x > 2$

26) $-\frac{11}{2} < x < \frac{1}{2}$

27) $\frac{2}{9} \le x \le 3$

28) $x \le \frac{1}{4} \text{ or } x \ge \frac{1}{2}$

29) $x < -1.5 \text{ or } x > \frac{2}{3}$

30) $-1 \le x \le -\frac{5}{18}$

31) $x \le -1 \text{ or } x \ge \frac{2}{17}$

32) $x \le -1 \text{ or } x \ge 3$

Graphing quadratic functions

1) $(-1, 2), x = -1$

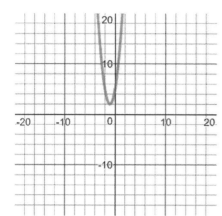

2) $(2, -4), x = 2$

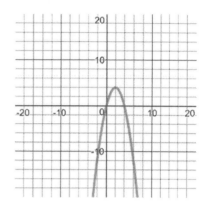

3) $(3, 8), x = 3$

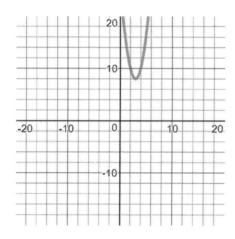

4) $(4, 3), x = 4$

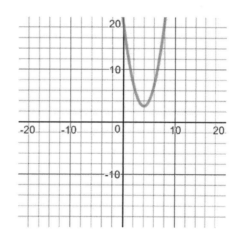

Chapter 5: Complex Numbers

Topics that you'll practice in this chapter:

- ✓ Adding and Subtracting Complex Numbers

- ✓ Multiplying and Dividing Complex Numbers

- ✓ Graphing Complex Numbers

- ✓ Rationalizing Imaginary Denominators

Mathematics is a hard thing to love. It has the unfortunate habit, like a rude dog, of turning its most unfavorable side towards you when you first make contact with it. — David Whiteland

Adding and Subtracting Complex Numbers

✍ *Simplify.*

1) $(2i) - (i) =$

2) $(2i) + (2i) =$

3) $(i) + (3i) =$

4) $(-2i) - (6i) =$

5) $(5i) + (4i) =$

6) $(3i) - (-7i) =$

7) $(-6i) + (-9i) =$

8) $(15i) - (7i) =$

9) $(-12i) - (5i) =$

10) $(2i) + (2 + 3i) =$

11) $(2 - 4i) + (-i) =$

12) $(-3i) + (3 + 5i) =$

13) $3 + (2 - 4i) =$

14) $(-5i) - (-5 + 2i) =$

15) $(5 + 3i) - (-4i) =$

16) $(8 + 5i) + (-7i) =$

17) $(9i) - (-6i + 10) =$

18) $(12i + 8) + (-7i) =$

19) $(13i) - (17 + 3i) =$

20) $(3 + 5i) + (8 + 3i) =$

21) $(8 - 3i) + (4 + i) =$

22) $(10 + 9i) + (6 + 8i) =$

23) $(-3 + 6i) - (-9 - i) =$

24) $(-5 + 15i) - (-3 + 3i) =$

25) $(-14 + i) - (-12 - 11i) =$

26) $(-18 - 3i) + (11 + 5i) =$

27) $(-11 - 9i) - (-9 - 3i) =$

28) $-8 + (2i) + (-8 + 6i) =$

29) $12 - (5i) + (4 - 14i) =$

30) $-2 + (-8 - 7i) - 9 =$

31) $(-12i) + (2 - 6i) + 10 =$

32) $(-8i) - (8 - 5i) + 6i =$

Multiplying and Dividing Complex Numbers

✍ *Simplify.*

1) $(5i)(-i) =$

2) $(-4i)(5i) =$

3) $(i)(7i)(-i) =$

4) $(3i)(-4i) =$

5) $(-2 - i)(4 + i) =$

6) $(2 - 2i)^2 =$

7) $(4 - 3i)(6 - 6i) =$

8) $(5 + 4i)^2 =$

9) $(4i)(- i)(2 - 5i) =$

10) $(2 - 8i)(3 - 5i) =$

11) $(-5 + 9i)(3 + 5i) =$

12) $(7 + 3i)(7 + 8i) =$

13) $2(3i) - (5i)(-8 + 5i) =$

14) $\dfrac{5}{-10i} =$

15) $\dfrac{4-3i}{-4i} =$

16) $\dfrac{5+9i}{i} =$

17) $\dfrac{12i}{-9+3i} =$

18) $\dfrac{-3-10}{5i} =$

19) $\dfrac{9i}{3-i} =$

20) $\dfrac{2+4i}{14+4i} =$

21) $\dfrac{5+6i}{-1+8i} =$

22) $\dfrac{-8-i}{-4-6i} =$

23) $\dfrac{-1+5i}{-8-7i} =$

24) $\dfrac{-2-9i}{-2+7i} =$

25) $\dfrac{4+i}{2-5i} =$

Graphing Complex Numbers

✍ *Identify each complex number graphed.*

1)

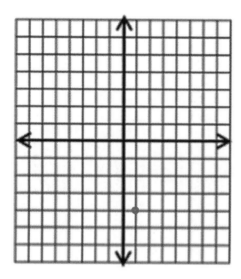

2)

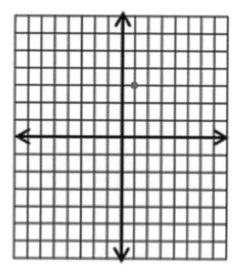

3)

4)

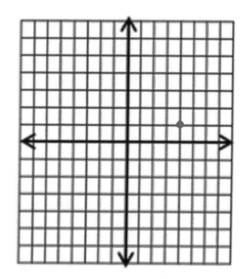

Rationalizing Imaginary Denominators

✎ *Simplify.*

1) $\dfrac{-2}{-2i} =$

2) $\dfrac{-1}{-9i} =$

3) $\dfrac{-8}{-5i} =$

4) $\dfrac{-5}{-i} =$

5) $\dfrac{3}{5i} =$

6) $\dfrac{6}{-4i} =$

7) $\dfrac{6}{-7i} =$

8) $\dfrac{-10}{3i} =$

9) $\dfrac{a}{bi} =$

10) $\dfrac{10-10}{-5i} =$

11) $\dfrac{4-9i}{-6i} =$

12) $\dfrac{6+8i}{9i} =$

13) $\dfrac{8i}{-1+3i} =$

14) $\dfrac{5i}{-2-6i} =$

15) $\dfrac{-10-5i}{-6+6i} =$

16) $\dfrac{-5-9i}{9+8i} =$

17) $\dfrac{-5-3i}{7-10i} =$

18) $\dfrac{-1+i}{-5i} =$

19) $\dfrac{-6-i}{i} =$

20) $\dfrac{-4-i}{9+5i} =$

21) $\dfrac{-3+i}{-2i} =$

22) $\dfrac{-6-i}{-1+6i} =$

23) $\dfrac{-9-3i}{-3+3i} =$

24) $\dfrac{4i+1}{-1+3i} =$

Answers of Worksheets – Chapter 5

Adding and Subtracting Complex Numbers

1) i
2) $4i$
3) $4i$
4) $-8i$
5) $9i$
6) $10i$
7) $-15i$
8) $8i$
9) $-17i$
10) $2 + 5i$
11) $2 - 5i$

12) $3 + 2i$
13) $5 - 4i$
14) $5 - 7i$
15) $5 + 7i$
16) $8 - 2i$
17) $10 + 15i$
18) $8 + 5i$
19) $-17 + 10i$
20) $11 + 8i$
21) $12 - 2i$
22) $16 + 17i$

23) $6 + 7i$
24) $-2 + 12i$
25) $-2 + 12i$
26) $-7 + 2i$
27) $-2 - 6i$
28) $-16 + 8i$
29) $16 - 19i$
30) $-19 - 7i$
31) $12 - 18i$
32) $-8 + 3i$

Multiplying and Dividing Complex Numbers

1) 5
2) 20
3) $7i$
4) 12
5) $-7 - 6i$
6) $-8i$
7) $6 - 42i$
8) $9 + 40i$
9) $8 - 20i$
10) $-34 - 34i$
11) $-60 + 2i$
12) $25 + 77i$

13) $25 + 46i$
14) $\dfrac{i}{2}$
15) $\dfrac{3}{4} + i$
16) $9 - 5i$
17) $\dfrac{2}{5} - \dfrac{6}{5}i$
18) $-2 + \dfrac{3}{5}i$
19) $-\dfrac{9}{10} + \dfrac{27}{10}i$
20) $\dfrac{11}{53} + \dfrac{12}{53}i$

21) $\dfrac{43}{65} - \dfrac{46}{65}i$
22) $\dfrac{19}{26} + \dfrac{11}{13}i$
23) $-\dfrac{27}{113} - \dfrac{47}{113}i$
24) $-\dfrac{59}{53} + \dfrac{32}{53}i$
25) $\dfrac{3}{29} + \dfrac{22}{29}i$

Graphing Complex Numbers

1) $1 - 4i$
2) $1 + 3i$

3) $2 + 4i$
4) $4 + i$

Rationalizing Imaginary Denominators

1) $-i$
2) $-\dfrac{1}{9}i$
3) $\dfrac{-8}{5}i$
4) $-5i$

5) $-\dfrac{3}{5}i$
6) $\dfrac{3}{2}i$
7) $\dfrac{6}{7}i$

8) $\dfrac{10}{3}i$
9) $-\dfrac{a}{b}i$
10) $2 + 2i$

11) $\frac{2}{3} + \frac{3}{2}i$

12) $\frac{6}{91} + \frac{8}{91}i$

13) $\frac{12}{5} - \frac{4}{5}i$

14) $-\frac{3}{4} - \frac{1}{4}i$

15) $\frac{5}{12} + \frac{5}{4}i$

16) $-\frac{117}{145} - \frac{41}{145}i$

17) $-\frac{5}{149} - \frac{71}{149}i$

18) $-\frac{1}{5} - \frac{1}{5}i$

19) $-1 + 6i$

20) $-\frac{41}{106} + \frac{11}{106}i$

21) $-\frac{1}{2} - \frac{3}{2}i$

22) i

23) $1 + 2i$

24) $\frac{11}{10} - \frac{7}{10}i$

Chapter 6: Matrices

Topics that you'll practice in this chapter:

- ✓ Adding and Subtracting Matrices

- ✓ Matrix Multiplications

- ✓ Finding Determinants of a Matrix

- ✓ Finding Inverse of a Matrix

- ✓ Matrix Equations

Mathematics is an independent world created out of pure intelligence.

— William Woods Worth

Adding and Subtracting Matrices

✎ **Simplify.**

1) $[2 \quad -5 \quad -3] + [1 \quad -2 \quad -3] =$

2) $[4 \quad 2] + [-2 \quad -6] =$

3) $\begin{bmatrix} 2 \\ 4 \end{bmatrix} + \begin{bmatrix} 5 \\ 6 \end{bmatrix} =$

4) $\begin{bmatrix} 8 & 7 \\ -6 & 5 \end{bmatrix} + \begin{bmatrix} 4 & -3 \\ 1 & 13 \end{bmatrix} =$

5) $[-13 \quad 18 \quad 12] + [34 \quad -3 \quad 9] =$

6) $\begin{bmatrix} 3 & 6 \\ -1 & -3 \\ -5 & -1 \end{bmatrix} + \begin{bmatrix} 0 & -1 \\ 6 & 0 \\ 2 & 3 \end{bmatrix} =$

7) $\begin{bmatrix} 6 & 8 \\ -14 & 33 \end{bmatrix} - \begin{bmatrix} 12 & 5 \\ -27 & -8 \end{bmatrix} =$

8) $\begin{bmatrix} 16 & -4 \\ -38 & 24 \end{bmatrix} + \begin{bmatrix} 9 & -6 \\ 5 & 2 \end{bmatrix} =$

9) $\begin{bmatrix} 12 & 21 \\ -17 & 33 \end{bmatrix} - \begin{bmatrix} 5 & -8 \\ 2 & 19 \end{bmatrix} =$

10) $\begin{bmatrix} 16 & -4 \\ -38 & 14 \end{bmatrix} + \begin{bmatrix} 9 & -6 \\ 5 & 2 \end{bmatrix} =$

11) $\begin{bmatrix} -5 & 2 & -2 \\ 4 & -2 & 0 \end{bmatrix} - \begin{bmatrix} 6 & -5 & -6 \\ 1 & 3 & -3 \end{bmatrix} =$

12) $\begin{bmatrix} -4n & n+m \\ -2n & -4m \end{bmatrix} + \begin{bmatrix} 4 & -5 \\ 3m & 0 \end{bmatrix} =$

13) $\begin{bmatrix} -6r+t \\ -r \\ 6s \end{bmatrix} + \begin{bmatrix} 6r \\ -4t \\ -3r+2 \end{bmatrix} =$

14) $\begin{bmatrix} z-5 \\ -6 \\ -1-6z \\ 3y \end{bmatrix} + \begin{bmatrix} -3y \\ 3z \\ 5+z \\ 4z \end{bmatrix} =$

15) $\begin{bmatrix} 2 & -5 & 9 \\ 4 & -7 & 11 \\ -6 & 3 & -17 \end{bmatrix} + \begin{bmatrix} 3 & 4 & -5 \\ 13 & 2 & 5 \\ 4 & -8 & 1 \end{bmatrix} =$

16) $\begin{bmatrix} 1 & -7 & 15 \\ 31 & 3 & 18 \\ 22 & 6 & 4 \end{bmatrix} + \begin{bmatrix} 13 & 17 & 5 \\ 3 & 8 & -1 \\ -9 & 2 & 12 \end{bmatrix} =$

Matrix Multiplication

✎ *Solve.*

1) $\begin{bmatrix} -5 \\ 6 \\ 0 \end{bmatrix} \begin{bmatrix} 3 & -1 \end{bmatrix} =$

2) $\begin{bmatrix} -5 & -5 \\ -1 & 2 \end{bmatrix} \begin{bmatrix} -2 & -3 \\ 3 & 5 \end{bmatrix} =$

3) $\begin{bmatrix} 3 & 2 \end{bmatrix} \begin{bmatrix} 0 & -6 \\ 6 & 2 \end{bmatrix} =$

4) $\begin{bmatrix} 3 & 2 & 5 \\ 2 & 3 & 1 \end{bmatrix} \begin{bmatrix} 4 & 5 & -5 \\ 5 & -1 & 6 \end{bmatrix} =$

5) $\begin{bmatrix} -4 & -y \\ -2x & -4 \end{bmatrix} \begin{bmatrix} -4x & 0 \\ 2y & -5 \end{bmatrix}$

6) $\begin{bmatrix} 2 & -5v \end{bmatrix} \begin{bmatrix} -5u & -v \\ 0 & 6 \end{bmatrix} =$

7) $\begin{bmatrix} -3 & 5 \\ -2 & 1 \end{bmatrix} \begin{bmatrix} 6 & -2 \\ 1 & -5 \end{bmatrix} =$

8) $\begin{bmatrix} -4 & -6 & -6 \\ 0 & 6 & 3 \end{bmatrix} \begin{bmatrix} 0 \\ -3 \\ 0 \end{bmatrix} =$

9) $\begin{bmatrix} 6 & -12 \\ 5 & 11 \end{bmatrix} \begin{bmatrix} 2 & 8 \\ 3 & 1 \end{bmatrix} =$

10) $\begin{bmatrix} -6 & -2 \end{bmatrix} \begin{bmatrix} 5 & -4 \\ -2 & 3 \end{bmatrix} =$

11) $\begin{bmatrix} 0 & 2 \\ -2 & -5 \end{bmatrix} \begin{bmatrix} 6 & -6 \\ 3 & 0 \end{bmatrix} =$

12) $\begin{bmatrix} 3 & -1 \\ -3 & 6 \\ -6 & -6 \end{bmatrix} \begin{bmatrix} -1 & 6 \\ 5 & 4 \end{bmatrix} =$

13) $\begin{bmatrix} 0 & 5 \\ -3 & 1 \\ -5 & 1 \end{bmatrix} \begin{bmatrix} -4 & 4 \\ -2 & -4 \end{bmatrix} =$

14) $\begin{bmatrix} 5 & 3 & 5 \\ 1 & 5 & 0 \end{bmatrix} \begin{bmatrix} -4 & 2 \\ -3 & 4 \\ 3 & -5 \end{bmatrix} =$

15) $\begin{bmatrix} 4 & 5 \\ -4 & 6 \\ -5 & -6 \end{bmatrix} \begin{bmatrix} 4 & 6 \\ 6 & 2 \\ -4 & 1 \end{bmatrix} =$

16) $\begin{bmatrix} -2 & -6 \\ -4 & 3 \\ 5 & 0 \\ 4 & -6 \end{bmatrix} \begin{bmatrix} 2 & -2 & 2 \\ -2 & 0 & -3 \end{bmatrix} =$

17) $\begin{bmatrix} -1 & 1 & -1 \\ 5 & 2 & -5 \\ 6 & -5 & 1 \\ -5 & 6 & 0 \end{bmatrix} \begin{bmatrix} 6 & 5 \\ 5 & -6 \\ 6 & 0 \end{bmatrix} =$

18) $\begin{bmatrix} 5 & 3 & 2 \\ 6 & 4 & 1 \\ 7 & -9 & 12 \end{bmatrix} \begin{bmatrix} -2 & 5 & 4 \\ 5 & 6 & 13 \\ 3 & 2 & 1 \end{bmatrix} =$

Finding Determinants of a Matrix

✍ *Evaluate the determinant of each matrix.*

1) $\begin{bmatrix} 0 & -4 \\ -6 & -2 \end{bmatrix} =$

2) $\begin{bmatrix} 5 & 3 \\ 6 & 6 \end{bmatrix} =$

3) $\begin{bmatrix} -4 & 7 \\ -2 & 9 \end{bmatrix} =$

4) $\begin{bmatrix} -1 & 1 \\ -1 & 4 \end{bmatrix} =$

5) $\begin{bmatrix} -9 & -9 \\ -7 & -10 \end{bmatrix} =$

6) $\begin{bmatrix} -1 & 8 \\ 5 & 0 \end{bmatrix} =$

7) $\begin{bmatrix} 2 & 5 \\ 3 & 8 \end{bmatrix} =$

8) $\begin{bmatrix} 8 & -6 \\ -10 & 9 \end{bmatrix} =$

9) $\begin{bmatrix} 2 & -2 \\ 7 & -7 \end{bmatrix} =$

10) $\begin{bmatrix} -5 & 0 \\ 3 & 10 \end{bmatrix} =$

11) $\begin{bmatrix} 0 & 6 \\ -6 & 0 \end{bmatrix} =$

12) $\begin{bmatrix} 3 & 4 \\ 2 & -6 \end{bmatrix} =$

13) $\begin{bmatrix} 8 & 5 \\ -4 & -6 \end{bmatrix} =$

14) $\begin{bmatrix} 0 & 4 \\ 6 & 5 \end{bmatrix} =$

15) $\begin{bmatrix} 6 & 1 & 7 \\ 2 & -3 & 3 \\ 4 & -1 & 2 \end{bmatrix} =$

16) $\begin{bmatrix} -2 & 5 & -4 \\ 0 & -3 & 5 \\ -5 & 5 & -6 \end{bmatrix} =$

17) $\begin{bmatrix} -3 & 1 & 8 \\ -9 & -1 & 7 \\ 0 & 2 & 1 \end{bmatrix} =$

18) $\begin{vmatrix} 5 & 3 & 3 \\ -4 & -5 & 1 \\ 5 & 3 & 0 \end{vmatrix} =$

19) $\begin{vmatrix} 6 & 2 & -1 \\ -5 & -4 & -5 \\ 3 & -3 & 1 \end{vmatrix} =$

20) $\begin{bmatrix} 6 & 5 & -3 \\ -5 & 4 & -2 \\ 1 & -4 & 5 \end{bmatrix} =$

21) $\begin{bmatrix} -1 & -8 & 9 \\ 4 & 12 & -7 \\ -10 & 3 & 2 \end{bmatrix} =$

22) $\begin{vmatrix} 3 & 9 & 1 \\ 2 & -10 & 1 \\ 5 & 3 & 8 \end{vmatrix} =$

23) $\begin{bmatrix} 6 & 4 & 2 \\ 3 & -7 & 1 \\ 5 & 5 & 3 \end{bmatrix} =$

24) $\begin{bmatrix} -1 & -8 & 9 \\ 4 & 12 & -7 \\ -10 & 3 & 2 \end{bmatrix} =$

25) $\begin{bmatrix} 5 & 4 & 7 \\ 3 & -6 & 5 \\ 4 & 2 & -3 \end{bmatrix} =$

26) $\begin{bmatrix} 3 & 4 & 1 \\ 2 & 5 & -2 \\ -1 & 6 & -3 \end{bmatrix} =$

27) $\begin{bmatrix} 4 & 2 & 6 \\ -1 & -4 & 5 \\ 3 & 7 & 2 \end{bmatrix} =$

28) $\begin{bmatrix} 3 & 5 & 1 \\ 1 & 4 & 2 \\ 7 & 1 & 9 \end{bmatrix} =$

Finding Inverse of a Matrix

✎ *Find the inverse of each matrix.*

1) $\begin{bmatrix} 2 & -1 \\ 0 & 3 \end{bmatrix} =$

2) $\begin{bmatrix} 3 & -1 \\ -1 & 4 \end{bmatrix} =$

3) $\begin{bmatrix} 5 & -2 \\ 1 & 3 \end{bmatrix} =$

4) $\begin{bmatrix} 6 & 2 \\ 4 & 1 \end{bmatrix} =$

5) $\begin{bmatrix} 4 & 2 \\ 2 & 6 \end{bmatrix} =$

6) $\begin{bmatrix} 8 & 2 \\ -2 & 4 \end{bmatrix} =$

7) $\begin{bmatrix} 5 & -1 \\ 3 & 2 \end{bmatrix} =$

8) $\begin{bmatrix} -2 & 2 \\ 3 & -1 \end{bmatrix} =$

9) $\begin{bmatrix} 5 & -3 \\ -3 & 5 \end{bmatrix} =$

10) $\begin{bmatrix} 3 & -2 \\ -4 & 6 \end{bmatrix} =$

11) $\begin{bmatrix} 5 & -8 \\ 6 & -9 \end{bmatrix} =$

12) $\begin{bmatrix} 2 & -10 \\ -11 & 8 \end{bmatrix} =$

13) $\begin{bmatrix} -9 & -6 \\ -5 & -4 \end{bmatrix} =$

14) $\begin{bmatrix} -3 & 3 \\ 8 & 7 \end{bmatrix} =$

15) $\begin{bmatrix} -2 & 2 \\ -9 & 8 \end{bmatrix} =$

16) $\begin{bmatrix} 3 & -2 \\ -4 & 6 \end{bmatrix} =$

17) $\begin{bmatrix} 9 & 2 \\ 3 & 1 \end{bmatrix} =$

18) $\begin{bmatrix} -3 & 1 \\ 9 & -1 \end{bmatrix} =$

19) $\begin{bmatrix} -6 & 11 \\ -4 & 7 \end{bmatrix} =$

20) $\begin{bmatrix} -1 & 7 \\ -1 & 7 \end{bmatrix} =$

21) $\begin{bmatrix} 1 & -1 \\ -6 & -3 \end{bmatrix} =$

22) $\begin{bmatrix} 11 & -5 \\ 2 & -1 \end{bmatrix} =$

23) $\begin{bmatrix} 0 & -2 \\ -1 & -9 \end{bmatrix} =$

24) $\begin{bmatrix} 0 & 0 \\ -6 & 4 \end{bmatrix} =$

25) $\begin{bmatrix} -9 & -9 \\ -2 & -2 \end{bmatrix} =$

26) $\begin{bmatrix} 3 & 4 \\ -5 & -7 \end{bmatrix} =$

27) $\begin{bmatrix} 4 & 5 \\ 3 & 3 \end{bmatrix} =$

28) $\begin{bmatrix} 3 & -4 \\ 0 & 10 \end{bmatrix} =$

29) $\begin{bmatrix} 3 & -10 \\ -2 & -1 \end{bmatrix} =$

30) $\begin{bmatrix} -4 & -5 \\ 6 & 11 \end{bmatrix} =$

Matrix Equations

✎ **Solve each equation for the unknown variables.**

1) $\begin{bmatrix} -1 & -9 \\ 0 & -1 \end{bmatrix} C = \begin{bmatrix} 11 \\ 2 \end{bmatrix}$

2) $\begin{bmatrix} -5 \\ 5 \\ -20 \end{bmatrix} = 5B$

3) $\begin{bmatrix} -1 & 2 \\ -6 & 10 \end{bmatrix} z = \begin{bmatrix} 6 \\ 22 \end{bmatrix}$

4) $3x = \begin{bmatrix} 12 & -12 \\ 21 & -27 \end{bmatrix}$

5) $A \times \begin{bmatrix} -3 & 6 \\ -6 & 12 \end{bmatrix} = \begin{bmatrix} -1 & 2 \\ -2 & 4 \end{bmatrix}$

6) $5x = \begin{bmatrix} 20 & -10 \\ 25 & -15 \end{bmatrix}$

7) $\begin{bmatrix} -1 & 2 \\ -6 & 10 \end{bmatrix} + \begin{bmatrix} a & b \\ c & d \end{bmatrix} = \begin{bmatrix} 3 & 0 \\ -3 & 6 \end{bmatrix}$

8) $-2x = \begin{bmatrix} -4 & -2 \\ 14 & 6 \end{bmatrix}$

9) $\begin{bmatrix} -1 & 2 \\ -6 & 10 \end{bmatrix} - x = \begin{bmatrix} 0 & 5 \\ -8 & 4 \end{bmatrix}$

10) $-4x = \begin{bmatrix} -8 & 40 & -28 \end{bmatrix}$

11) $\begin{bmatrix} 20 & -3 \\ 15 & -3 \end{bmatrix} = \begin{bmatrix} -6 & -5 \\ -5 & -4 \end{bmatrix} x$

12) $y - \begin{bmatrix} -1 \\ -5 \\ 8 \\ 8 \end{bmatrix} = \begin{bmatrix} -6 \\ 6 \\ -16 \\ 0 \end{bmatrix}$

13) $\begin{bmatrix} -25 \\ 37 \\ 21 \end{bmatrix} - 6x = \begin{bmatrix} -1 \\ -5 \\ -3 \end{bmatrix}$

14) $\begin{bmatrix} -1 & -2 \\ 2 & 9 \end{bmatrix} B = \begin{bmatrix} -3 & -5 & 13 \\ 21 & 0 & -36 \end{bmatrix}$

15) $\begin{bmatrix} -1 & 1 \\ 5 & -2 \end{bmatrix} C = \begin{bmatrix} 4 \\ -26 \end{bmatrix}$

16) $\begin{bmatrix} 4 & -2 \\ -7 & 2 \end{bmatrix} C = \begin{bmatrix} -6 \\ 12 \end{bmatrix}$

17) $\begin{bmatrix} 2 & -3 \\ -5 & 5 \end{bmatrix} z = \begin{bmatrix} -1 \\ 20 \end{bmatrix}$

18) $\begin{bmatrix} -10 \\ 4 \\ 3 \end{bmatrix} = y - \begin{bmatrix} 7 \\ -5 \\ -11 \end{bmatrix}$

19) $-4b - \begin{bmatrix} 5 \\ 2 \\ -6 \end{bmatrix} = \begin{bmatrix} -33 \\ -2 \\ -22 \end{bmatrix}$

20) $\begin{bmatrix} -3 & -1 \\ -27 & -18 \end{bmatrix} + 4p = \begin{bmatrix} -7 & 3 \\ -3 & -2 \end{bmatrix}$

Answers of Worksheets – Chapter 6

Adding and Subtracting Matrices

1) $[3 \quad -7 \quad -6]$

2) $[2 \quad -4]$

3) $\begin{bmatrix} 7 \\ 10 \end{bmatrix}$

4) $\begin{bmatrix} 12 & 4 \\ -5 & 18 \end{bmatrix}$

5) $[21 \quad 15 \quad 21]$

6) $\begin{bmatrix} 3 & 5 \\ 5 & -3 \\ -3 & 2 \end{bmatrix}$

7) $\begin{bmatrix} -6 & 3 \\ 13 & 41 \end{bmatrix}$

8) $\begin{bmatrix} 25 & -10 \\ -33 & 16 \end{bmatrix}$

9) $\begin{bmatrix} 7 & 29 \\ -19 & 14 \end{bmatrix}$

10) $\begin{bmatrix} 25 & -10 \\ -33 & 16 \end{bmatrix}$

11) $\begin{bmatrix} -11 & 7 & 4 \\ 3 & -5 & 3 \end{bmatrix}$

12) $\begin{bmatrix} -4n+4 & n+m-5 \\ -2n+3m & -4m \end{bmatrix}$

13) $\begin{bmatrix} t \\ -r-4t \\ 6s-3r+2 \end{bmatrix}$

14) $\begin{bmatrix} z-5-3y \\ -6+3z \\ -4-5z \\ 3y+4z \end{bmatrix}$

15) $\begin{bmatrix} -1 & -9 & 14 \\ -9 & -9 & 6 \\ -6 & 11 & -18 \end{bmatrix}$

16) $\begin{bmatrix} 14 & 10 & 20 \\ 34 & 11 & 17 \\ 13 & 8 & 16 \end{bmatrix}$

Matrix Multiplication

1) $\begin{bmatrix} -15 & 5 \\ 18 & -6 \\ 0 & 0 \end{bmatrix}$

2) $\begin{bmatrix} -5 & -10 \\ 8 & 13 \end{bmatrix}$

3) $[12 \quad -14]$

4) Undefined

5) $\begin{bmatrix} 16x - 2y^2 & 5y \\ 8x^2 - 8y & 20 \end{bmatrix}$

6) $\begin{bmatrix} -10u & -32v \end{bmatrix}$

7) $\begin{bmatrix} -13 & -19 \\ -11 & -1 \end{bmatrix}$

8) $\begin{bmatrix} 18 \\ -18 \end{bmatrix}$

9) $\begin{bmatrix} -24 & 36 \\ 43 & 51 \end{bmatrix}$

10) $\begin{bmatrix} -26 & 18 \end{bmatrix}$

11) $\begin{bmatrix} 6 & 0 \\ -27 & 12 \end{bmatrix}$

12) $\begin{bmatrix} -8 & 14 \\ 33 & 6 \\ -24 & -60 \end{bmatrix}$

13) $\begin{bmatrix} -10 & -20 \\ 10 & -16 \\ 18 & -24 \end{bmatrix}$

14) $\begin{bmatrix} -14 & -3 \\ -19 & 22 \end{bmatrix}$

15) Undefined

16) $\begin{bmatrix} 8 & 4 & 14 \\ -14 & 8 & -17 \\ 10 & -10 & 10 \\ 20 & -8 & 26 \end{bmatrix}$

17) $\begin{bmatrix} -7 & -11 \\ 10 & 13 \\ 17 & 60 \\ 0 & -61 \end{bmatrix}$

18) $\begin{bmatrix} 11 & 47 & 61 \\ 11 & 56 & 77 \\ -23 & 5 & -77 \end{bmatrix}$

Finding Determinants of a Matrix

1) −24

2) 12

3) −22

4) −3

5) 27

6) −40

7) 1

8) 12

9) 0

10) −50

11) −36

12) −26

13) −28

14) −24

15) 60

16) −51

17) −102

18) 39

19) −161

20) 139

21) 647

22) −292

23) −72

24) 647

25) 366

27) −108

26) 40

28) 100

Finding Inverse of a Matrix

1) $\begin{bmatrix} \frac{1}{2} & \frac{1}{6} \\ 0 & \frac{1}{3} \end{bmatrix}$

2) $\begin{bmatrix} \frac{4}{11} & \frac{1}{11} \\ \frac{1}{11} & \frac{3}{11} \end{bmatrix}$

3) $\begin{bmatrix} \frac{3}{17} & \frac{2}{17} \\ -\frac{1}{17} & \frac{5}{17} \end{bmatrix}$

4) $\begin{bmatrix} -\frac{1}{2} & 1 \\ 2 & -3 \end{bmatrix}$

5) $\begin{bmatrix} \frac{3}{10} & -\frac{1}{10} \\ -\frac{1}{10} & \frac{1}{5} \end{bmatrix}$

6) $\begin{bmatrix} \frac{1}{9} & -\frac{1}{18} \\ \frac{1}{18} & \frac{2}{9} \end{bmatrix}$

7) $\begin{bmatrix} \frac{2}{13} & \frac{1}{13} \\ -\frac{3}{13} & \frac{5}{13} \end{bmatrix}$

8) $\begin{bmatrix} \frac{1}{4} & \frac{1}{2} \\ \frac{3}{4} & \frac{1}{2} \end{bmatrix}$

9) $\begin{bmatrix} \frac{5}{16} & \frac{3}{16} \\ \frac{3}{16} & \frac{5}{16} \end{bmatrix}$

10) $\begin{bmatrix} \frac{3}{5} & \frac{1}{5} \\ \frac{2}{5} & \frac{3}{10} \end{bmatrix}$

11) $\begin{bmatrix} -3 & \frac{8}{3} \\ -2 & \frac{5}{3} \end{bmatrix}$

12) $\begin{bmatrix} -\frac{4}{47} & -\frac{5}{47} \\ -\frac{2}{94} & -\frac{1}{47} \end{bmatrix}$

13) $\begin{bmatrix} -\frac{2}{3} & 1 \\ \frac{5}{6} & -\frac{3}{2} \end{bmatrix}$

14) $\begin{bmatrix} -\frac{7}{45} & \frac{1}{15} \\ \frac{8}{45} & \frac{1}{15} \end{bmatrix}$

15) $\begin{bmatrix} 4 & -1 \\ \frac{9}{2} & -1 \end{bmatrix}$

16) $\begin{bmatrix} \frac{3}{5} & \frac{1}{5} \\ \frac{2}{5} & \frac{3}{10} \end{bmatrix}$

17) $\begin{bmatrix} \frac{1}{6} & \frac{1}{6} \\ \frac{3}{2} & \frac{1}{3} \end{bmatrix}$

18) $\begin{bmatrix} \frac{1}{3} & \frac{-2}{3} \\ -1 & 3 \end{bmatrix}$

19) $\begin{bmatrix} \frac{7}{2} & -\frac{11}{2} \\ 2 & -3 \end{bmatrix}$

20) No inverse exists

21) $\begin{bmatrix} \frac{1}{3} & -\frac{1}{9} \\ -\frac{2}{3} & -\frac{1}{9} \end{bmatrix}$

22) $\begin{bmatrix} 1 & -5 \\ 2 & -11 \end{bmatrix}$

23) $\begin{bmatrix} \frac{9}{2} & -1 \\ -\frac{1}{2} & 0 \end{bmatrix}$

24) No inverse exists

25) No inverse exists

26) $\begin{bmatrix} 7 & 4 \\ -5 & -3 \end{bmatrix}$

27) $\begin{bmatrix} -1 & \frac{5}{3} \\ 1 & \frac{-4}{3} \end{bmatrix}$

28) $\begin{bmatrix} \frac{1}{3} & \frac{2}{15} \\ 0 & \frac{1}{10} \end{bmatrix}$

29) $\begin{bmatrix} \frac{1}{23} & -\frac{10}{23} \\ -\frac{2}{23} & -\frac{3}{23} \end{bmatrix}$

30) $\begin{bmatrix} -\frac{11}{14} & -\frac{5}{14} \\ \frac{3}{7} & \frac{2}{7} \end{bmatrix}$

Matrix Equations

1) $\begin{bmatrix} 7 \\ -2 \end{bmatrix}$

2) $\begin{bmatrix} -1 \\ 1 \\ -4 \end{bmatrix}$

3) $\begin{bmatrix} 8 \\ 7 \end{bmatrix}$

4) $\begin{bmatrix} 4 & -4 \\ 7 & -9 \end{bmatrix}$

5) $A = \frac{1}{3}$

6) $\begin{bmatrix} 4 & -2 \\ 5 & -3 \end{bmatrix}$

7) $\begin{bmatrix} 4 & -2 \\ 3 & -4 \end{bmatrix}$

8) $\begin{bmatrix} 2 & 1 \\ -7 & -3 \end{bmatrix}$

9) $\begin{bmatrix} -1 & -3 \\ 2 & 6 \end{bmatrix}$

10) $\begin{bmatrix} 2 & -10 & 7 \end{bmatrix}$

11) $\begin{bmatrix} 5 & 3 \\ -10 & -3 \end{bmatrix}$

12) $\begin{bmatrix} -7 \\ 1 \\ -8 \\ 8 \end{bmatrix}$

13) $\begin{bmatrix} -4 \\ 7 \\ 4 \end{bmatrix}$

14) $\begin{bmatrix} -3 & 9 & -9 \\ 3 & -2 & -2 \end{bmatrix}$

15) $\begin{bmatrix} -6 \\ -2 \end{bmatrix}$

16) $\begin{bmatrix} -2 \\ -1 \end{bmatrix}$

17) $\begin{bmatrix} -11 \\ -7 \end{bmatrix}$

18) $\begin{bmatrix} -3 \\ -1 \\ -8 \end{bmatrix}$

19) $\begin{bmatrix} 7 \\ 0 \\ 7 \end{bmatrix}$

20) $\begin{bmatrix} -1 & 1 \\ 6 & 4 \end{bmatrix}$

Chapter 7: Polynomial Operations

Topics that you'll practice in this chapter:

- ✓ Writing Polynomials in Standard Form
- ✓ Simplifying Polynomials
- ✓ Adding and Subtracting Polynomials
- ✓ Multiplying Monomials
- ✓ Multiplying and Dividing Monomials
- ✓ Multiplying a Polynomial and a Monomial
- ✓ Multiplying Binomials
- ✓ Factoring Trinomials
- ✓ Operations with Polynomials

Mathematics is the supreme judge; from its decisions there is no appeal.— Tobias Dantzig

Writing Polynomials in Standard Form

✎ *Write each polynomial in standard form.*

1) $9x - 7x =$

2) $-3 + 16x - 16x =$

3) $3x^2 - 5x^3 =$

4) $3 + 4x^3 - 3 =$

5) $2x^2 + 1x - 6x^3 =$

6) $-x^2 + 2x^3 =$

7) $2x + 4x^3 - 2x^2 =$

8) $-2x^2 + 4x - 6x^3 =$

9) $2x^2 + 2 - 5x =$

10) $12 - 7x + 9x^4 =$

11) $5x^2 + 13x - 2x^3 =$

12) $10 + 6x^2 - x^3 =$

13) $12x^2 - 7x + 9x^3 =$

14) $5x^4 - 3x^2 - 2x^3 =$

15) $-12 + 3x^2 - 6x^4 =$

16) $5x^2 - 9x^5 + 8x^3 - 11 =$

17) $4x^2 - 2x^5 + 14 - 7x^4 =$

18) $-x^2 + 2x - 5x^3 - 4x =$

19) $8x^5 + 11x^3 - 6x^5 - 8x^2 =$

20) $5x^2 - 12x^4 + 4x^2 + 5x^3 =$

21) $7x^3 - 6x^4 - 3x^2 + 22x^3 =$

22) $9x^2 + x^4 + 12x^3 - 5x^4 =$

23) $3x(2x + 5 - 2x^2) =$

24) $11x(x^5 + 2x^3) =$

25) $5x(3x^2 + 2x + 1) =$

26) $7x(3 - x + 6x^3) =$

27) $2x(3x^2 - 4x^4 + 3) =$

28) $6x(4x^5 + 7x^3 - 2) =$

29) $5x(3x^2 + 2x^3 + x) =$

30) $7x(3x - x^2 + 6x^4) =$

Simplifying Polynomials

✎ *Simplify each expression.*

1) $5(2x - 10) =$

2) $2x(4x - 2) =$

3) $4x(5x - 3) =$

4) $3x(7x + 3) =$

5) $4x(8x - 4) =$

6) $5x(5x + 4) =$

7) $(2x - 3)(x - 4) =$

8) $(x - 5)(3x + 4) =$

9) $(x - 5)(x - 3) =$

10) $(3x + 8)(3x - 8) =$

11) $(3x - 8)(3x - 4) =$

12) $3x^2 + 3x^2 - 2x^3 =$

13) $2x - x^2 + 6x^3 + 4 =$

14) $5x + 2x^2 - 9x^3 =$

15) $7x^2 + 5x^4 - 2x^3 =$

16) $-3x^2 + 5x^3 + 6x^4 =$

17) $-8x^2 + 2x^3 - 10x^4 + 5x =$

18) $11 - 6x^2 + 5x^2 - 12x^3 + 22 =$

19) $2x^2 - 2x + 3x^3 + 12x - 22x =$

20) $11 - 4x^2 + 3x^2 - 7x^3 + 3 =$

21) $2x^5 - x^3 + 8x^2 - 2x^5 =$

22) $(2x^3 - 1) + (3x^3 - 2x^3) =$

23) $3(4x^4 - 4x^3 - 5x^4) =$

24) $-5(x^6 + 10) - 8(14 - x^6) =$

25) $3x^2 - 5x^3 - x + 10 - 2x^2 =$

26) $11 - 3x^2 + 2x^2 - 5x^3 + 7 =$

27) $(8x^2 - 3x) - (5x - 5 - 8x^2) =$

28) $3x^2 - 5x^3 - x(2x^2 + 4x) =$

29) $4x + 8x^3 - 4 - 3(x^3 - 2) =$

30) $12 + 2x^2 - (8x^3 - x^2 + 6x^3) =$

31) $-2(x^4 + 6) - 5(10 + x^4) =$

32) $(8x^3 - 2x) - (5x - 2x^3) =$

Adding and Subtracting Polynomials

✍ *Add or subtract expressions.*

1) $(-x^2 - 2) + (2x^2 + 1) =$

2) $(2x^2 + 3) - (3 - 4x^2) =$

3) $(2x^3 + 3x^2) - (x^3 + 8) =$

4) $(4x^3 - x^2) + (3x^2 - 5x) =$

5) $(7x^3 + 9x) - (3x^3 + 2) =$

6) $(2x^3 - 2) + (2x^3 + 2) =$

7) $(4x^3 + 5) - (7 - 2x^3) =$

8) $(4x^2 + 2x^3) - (2x^3 + 5) =$

9) $(4x^2 - x) + (3x - 5x^2) =$

10) $(7x + 9) - (3x + 9) =$

11) $(4x^4 - 2x) - (6x - 2x^4) =$

12) $(12x - 4x^3) - (8x^3 + 6x) =$

13) $(2x^3 - 8x^2) - (5x^2 - 3x) =$

14) $(2x^2 - 6) + (9x^2 - 4x^3) =$

15) $(4x^3 + 3x^4) - (x^4 - 5x^3) =$

16) $(-2x^3 - 2x) + (6x - 2x^3) =$

17) $(2x - 4x^4) - (8x^4 + 3x) =$

18) $(2x - 8x^2) - (5x^4 - 3x^2) =$

19) $(2x^3 - 6) + (9x^3 - 4x^2) =$

20) $(4x^3 + 3x^4) - (x^4 - 5x^3) =$

21) $(-2x^2 + 10x^4 + x^3) + (4x^3 + 3x^4 + 8x^2) =$

22) $(3x^2 - 6x^5 - 2x) - (-2x^2 - 6x^5 + 2x) =$

23) $(5x + 9x^3 - 3x^5) + (8x^3 + 3x^5 - 2x) =$

24) $(3x^5 - 2x^4 - 4x) - (4x^2 + 10x^4 - 3x) =$

25) $(13x^2 - 6x^5 - 2x) - (-10x^2 - 11x^5 + 9x) =$

26) $(-12x^4 + 10x^5 + 2x^3) + (14x^3 + 23x^5 + 8x^4) =$

Multiplying Monomials

✎ *Simplify each expression.*

1) $4u^9 \times (-2u^3) =$

2) $(-2p^7) \times (-3p^2) =$

3) $3xy^2z^3 \times 2z^2 =$

4) $5u^5t \times 3ut^2 =$

5) $(-9a^6) \times (-5a^2b^4) =$

6) $-2a^3b^2 \times 4a^2b =$

7) $2xy^2 \times x^2y^3 =$

8) $3p^2q^4 \times (-2pq^3) =$

9) $4s^5t^2 \times 4st^3 =$

10) $(-6x^3y^2) \times 3x^2y =$

11) $2xy^2z \times 4z^2 =$

12) $4xy \times x^2y =$

13) $4pq^3 \times (-2p^4q) =$

14) $8s^4t^2 \times st^5 =$

15) $12p^3 \times (-3p^4) =$

16) $(-4p^2q^3r) \times 6pq^2r^3 =$

17) $(-8a^4) \times -12a^6b) =$

18) $3u^4v^2 \times (-7u^2v^3) =$

19) $4u^3 \times (-2u) =$

20) $-6xy^2 \times 3x^2y =$

21) $12y^2z^3 \times (-y^2z) =$

22) $5a^2bc^2 \times 2abc^2 =$

23) $(-7p^3q^5) \times (-4p^2q^3) =$

24) $4u^5v^2 \times (-8u^3v^2) =$

25) $12y^3z^4 \times (-y^6z) =$

26) $(-4pq^5r^3) \times 6p^2q^4r =$

27) $5ab^4c^2 \times 2a^5bc^2 =$

28) $2x^4yz^3 \times 3x^2y^4z^2 =$

Multiplying and Dividing Monomials

✎ **Simplify each expression.**

1) $(2x^2)(x^3) =$

2) $(3x^4)(2x^4) =$

3) $(6x^5)(2x^2) =$

4) $(4x^3)(3x^5) =$

5) $(15x^4)(3x^9) =$

6) $(2yx^2)(3y^2x^3) =$

7) $(2x^2y)(x^2y^3) =$

8) $(-2x^3y^4)(3x^3y^2) =$

9) $(-5x^3y^2)(-2x^4y^5) =$

10) $(9x^5y)(-3x^3y^3) =$

11) $(8x^7y^2)(6x^5y^4) =$

12) $(7x^4y^6)(4x^3y^4) =$

13) $(12x^2y^9)(7x^9y^{12}) =$

14) $(6x^2y^5)(5x^3y^2) =$

15) $(9x^2y^9)(4x^{10}y^9) =$

16) $(-10x^4y^8)(2x^9y^5) =$

17) $\dfrac{4x^2y^3}{xy^2} =$

18) $\dfrac{2x^4y^3}{2x^3y} =$

19) $\dfrac{8x^2y^2}{4x} =$

20) $\dfrac{6x^3y^4}{2x^2y^3} =$

21) $\dfrac{12\ ^6y^8}{4x^4y^2} =$

22) $\dfrac{26\ ^9y^5}{2x^3y^4} =$

23) $\dfrac{80x^{12}y^9}{10\ ^6y^7} =$

24) $\dfrac{95\ ^{18}y^7}{5x^9y^2} =$

25) $\dfrac{200x^3y^8}{40x^3y^7} =$

26) $\dfrac{-15x^{17}y^{13}}{3x^6y^9} =$

27) $\dfrac{-64x^8y^{10}}{8x^3y^7} =$

Multiplying a Polynomial and a Monomial

✎ *Find each product.*

1) $x(x + 3) =$

2) $8(2 - x) =$

3) $2x(2x + 1) =$

4) $x(-x + 3) =$

5) $3x(3x - 2) =$

6) $5(3x - 6y) =$

7) $8x(7x - 4) =$

8) $3x(9x + 2y) =$

9) $6x(x + 2y) =$

10) $9x(2x + 4y) =$

11) $12x(3x + 9) =$

12) $11x(2x - 11y) =$

13) $2x(6x - 6y) =$

14) $2x(3x - 6y + 3) =$

15) $5x(3x^2 + 2y^2) =$

16) $13x(4x + 8y) =$

17) $5(2x^2 - 9y^2) =$

18) $3x(-2x^2y + 3y) =$

19) $-2(2x^2 - 2xy + 2) =$

20) $3(x^2 - 4xy - 8) =$

21) $2x(2x^2 - 3xy + 2x) =$

22) $-x(-x^2 - 5x + 4xy) =$

23) $9(x^2 + xy - 8y^2) =$

24) $3x(2x^2 - 3x + 8) =$

25) $20(2x^2 - 8x - 5) =$

26) $x^2(-x^2 + 3x + 7) =$

27) $x^3(x^2 + 12 - 2x) =$

28) $6x^3(3x^2 - 2x + 2) =$

29) $8x^2(3x^2 - 5xy + 7y^2) =$

30) $2x^2(3x^2 - 5x + 12) =$

31) $2x^3(2x^2 + 5x - 4) =$

32) $5x(6x^2 - 5xy + 2y^2) =$

Multiplying Binomials

✎ *Find each product.*

1) $(x + 2)(x + 2) =$

2) $(x - 3)(x + 2) =$

3) $(x - 2)(x - 4) =$

4) $(x + 3)(x + 2) =$

5) $(x - 4)(x - 5) =$

6) $(x + 5)(x + 2) =$

7) $(x - 6)(x + 3) =$

8) $(x - 8)(x - 4) =$

9) $(x + 2)(x + 8) =$

10) $(x - 2)(x + 4) =$

11) $(x + 4)(x + 4) =$

12) $(x + 5)(x + 5) =$

13) $(x - 3)(x + 3) =$

14) $(x - 2)(x + 2) =$

15) $(x + 3)(x + 3) =$

16) $(x + 4)(x + 6) =$

17) $(x - 7)(x + 7) =$

18) $(x - 7)(x + 2) =$

19) $(2x + 2)(x + 3) =$

20) $(2x - 3)(2x + 4) =$

21) $(x - 8)(2x + 8) =$

22) $(x - 7)(x - 6) =$

23) $(x - 8)(x + 8) =$

24) $(3x - 2)(4x + 2) =$

25) $(2x - 5)(x + 7) =$

26) $(5x - 4)(3x + 3) =$

27) $(6x + 9)(4x + 9) =$

28) $(2x - 6)(5x + 6) =$

29) $(x + 4)(4x - 8) =$

30) $(6x - 4)(6x + 4) =$

31) $(3x + 3)(3x - 4) =$

32) $(x^2 + 2)(x^2 - 2) =$

Factoring Trinomials

✎ *Factor each trinomial.*

1) $x^2 + 8x + 15 =$

2) $x^2 - 5x + 6 =$

3) $x^2 + 6x + 8 =$

4) $x^2 - 6x + 8 =$

5) $x^2 - 8x + 16 =$

6) $x^2 - 7x + 12 =$

7) $x^2 + 11x + 18 =$

8) $x^2 + 2x - 24 =$

9) $x^2 + 4x - 12 =$

10) $x^2 - 10x + 9 =$

11) $x^2 + 5x - 14 =$

12) $x^2 - 6x - 27 =$

13) $x^2 - 11x - 42 =$

14) $x^2 + 22x + 121 =$

15) $6x^2 + x - 12 =$

16) $x^2 - 17x + 30 =$

17) $3x^2 + 11x - 4 =$

18) $10x^2 + 33x - 7 =$

19) $x^2 + 24x + 144 =$

20) $8x^2 + 10x - 3 =$

✎ *Solve each problem.*

21) The area of a rectangle is $x^2 + 2x - 24$. If the width of rectangle is $x - 4$, what is its length? _____

22) The area of a parallelogram is $8x^2 + 2x - 6$ and its height is $2x + 2$. What is the base of the parallelogram? _____

23) The area of a rectangle is $18x^2 + 9x - 2$. If the width of the rectangle is $6x - 1$, what is its length? _____

Operations with Polynomials

✎ *Find each product.*

1) $9(6x + 2) =$ _____

2) $8(3x + 7) =$ _____

3) $5(6x - 1) =$ _____

4) $-3(8x - 3) =$ _____

5) $3x^2(6x - 5) =$ _____

6) $5x^2(7x - 2) =$ _____

7) $6x^3(-3x + 4) =$ _____

8) $-7x^4(2x - 4) =$ _____

9) $8(x^2 + 2x - 3) =$ _____

10) $4(4x^2 - 2x + 1) =$ _____

11) $2(3x^2 + 2x - 2) =$ _____

12) $8x(5x^2 + 3x + 8) =$ _____

13) $(9x + 1)(3x - 1) =$ _____

14) $(4x + 5)(6x - 5) =$ _____

15) $(7x + 3)(5x - 6) =$ _____

16) $(3x - 4)(3x + 8) =$ _____

✎ *Solve each problem.*

17) *The measures of two sides of a triangle are* $(2x + 3y)$ *and* $(5x - 2y)$. *If the perimeter of the triangle is* $(12x + 5y)$, *what is the measure of the third side?*

    _____

18) *The height of a triangle is* $(4x + 5)$ *and its base is* $(2x - 2)$. *What is the area of the triangle?* _____

19) *One side of a square is* $(6x + 9)$. *What is the area of the square?* _____

20) *The length of a rectangle is* $(5x - 2y)$ *and its width is* $(12x + 2y)$. *What is the perimeter of the rectangle?* _____

21) *The side of a cube measures* $(x + 2)$. *What is the volume of the cube?* _____

22) *If the perimeter of a rectangle is* $(16x + 8y)$ *and its width is* $(2x + y)$, *what is the length of the rectangle?* _____

Answers of Worksheets – Chapter 7

Writing Polynomials in Standard Form

1) $2x$
2) -3
3) $-5x^3 + 3x^3$
4) $4x^3$
5) $-6x^3 + 2x^3 + x$
6) $2x^3 - x^2$
7) $4x^3 - 2x^2 + 2x$
8) $-6x^3 - 2x^2 + 4x$
9) $2x^2 - 5x + 2$
10) $9x^4 - 7x + 12$
11) $-2x^3 + 5x^2 + 13x$
12) $-x^3 + 6x^2 + 10$
13) $9x^3 + 12x^2 - 7x$
14) $5x^4 - 2x^3 - 3x^2$
15) $-6x^4 + 3x^2 - 12$

16) $-9x^5 + 8x^3 + 5x^2 - 11$
17) $-2x^5 - 7x^4 + 4x^2 + 14$
18) $-5x^3 - x^2 - 2x$
19) $2x^5 + 11x^3 - 8x^2$
20) $-12x^4 + 5x^3 + 9x^2$
21) $-6x^4 + 29x^3 - 3x^2$
22) $-4x^4 + 12x^3 + 9x^2$
23) $-6x^3 + 6x^2 + 15x$
24) $11x^6 + 22x^4$
25) $15x^3 + 10x^2 + 5x$
26) $42x^4 - 7x^2 + 21x$
27) $-8x^5 + 6x^3 + 6x$
28) $24x^6 + 42x^4 - 12x$
29) $10x^4 + 15x^3 + 5x^2$
30) $42x^5 - 7x^3 + 21x^2$

Simplifying Polynomials

1) $10x - 50$
2) $8x^2 - 4x$
3) $20x^2 - 12x$
4) $21x^2 + 9x$
5) $32x^2 - 16x$
6) $25x^2 + 20x$
7) $2x^2 - 11x + 12$
8) $3x^2 - 11x - 20$
9) $x^2 - 8x + 15$
10) $9x^2 - 64$
11) $9x^2 - 36x + 32$
12) $-2x^3 + 6x^2$
13) $6x^3 - x^2 + 2x + 4$
14) $-9x^3 + 2x^2 + 5x$
15) $5x^4 - 2x^3 + 7x^2$
16) $6x^4 + 5x^3 - 3x^2$

17) $-10x^4 + 2x^3 - 8x^2 + 5x$
18) $-12x^3 - x^2 + 33$
19) $3x^3 + 2x^2 - 12x$
20) $-7x^3 - x^2 + 14$
21) $-x^3 + 8x^2$
22) $3x^3 - 1$
23) $-3x^4 - 12x^3$
24) $3x^6 - 162$
25) $-5x^3 + x^2 - x + 10$
26) $-5x^3 - x^2 + 18$
27) $16x^2 - 8x + 5$
28) $-5x^3 - x^2$
29) $5x^3 + 4x + 2$
30) $-14x^3 + 3x^2 + 12$
31) $-7x^4 - 62$
32) $10x^3 - 7x$

Adding and Subtracting Polynomials

1) $x^2 - 1$
2) $6x^2$
3) $x^3 + 3x^2 - 8$
4) $4x^3 + 2x^2 - 5x$
5) $4x^3 + 9x - 2$
6) $4x^3$
7) $6x^3 - 2$
8) $4x^2 - 5$
9) $-x^2 + 2x$
10) $4x$
11) $6x^4 - 8x$
12) $-12x^3 + 6x$
13) $2x^3 - 13x^2 + 3x$

14) $-4x^3 + 11x^2 - 6$
15) $2x^4 + 9x^3$
16) $-4x^3 + 4x$
17) $-12x^4 - x$
18) $-5x^4 - 5x^2 + 2x$
19) $11x^3 - 4x^2 - 6$
20) $2x^4 + 9x^3$
21) $13x^4 + 5x^3 + 6x^2$
22) $5x^2 - 4x$
23) $17x^3 + 3x$
24) $3x^5 - 12x^4 - 4x^2 - x$
25) $5x^5 + 23x^2 - 11x$
26) $33x^5 - 4x^4 + 16x^3$

Multiplying Monomials

1) $-8u^{12}$
2) $6p^9$
3) $6xy^2z^5$
4) $15u^6t^3$
5) $45a^8b^4$
6) $-8a^5b^3$
7) $2x^3y^5$
8) $-6p^3q^7$
9) $16s^6t^5$
10) $-18x^5y^3$
11) $8xy^2z^3$

12) $4x^3y^2$
13) $-8p^5q^4$
14) $8s^5t^7$
15) $-36p^7$
16) $-24p^3q^4r^4$
17) $96a^{10}b$
18) $-21u^6v^5$
19) $-8u^4$
20) $-18x^3y^3$

21) $-12y^4z^4$
22) $10a^3b^2c^4$
23) $28p^5q^8$
24) $-32u^8v^4$
25) $-12y^9z^5$
26) $-24p^3q^9r^4$
27) $10a^6b^5c^4$
28) $6x^6y^5z^5$

Multiplying and Dividing Monomials

1) $2x^5$
2) $6x^8$
3) $12x^7$
4) $12x^8$
5) $45x^{13}$
6) $6x^5y^3$
7) $2x^4y^4$
8) $-6x^6y^6$

9) $10x^7y^7$
10) $-27x^8y^4$
11) $48x^{12}y^6$
12) $28x^7y^{10}$
13) $84x^{11}y^{21}$
14) $30x^5y^7$
15) $36x^{12}y^{18}$
16) $-20x^{13}y^{13}$

17) $4xy$
18) xy^2
19) $2xy$
20) $3xy$
21) $3x^2y^6$
22) $13x^6y$
23) $8x^6y^2$
24) $19x^9y^5$

25) $5y$ 26) $-5x^{11}y^4$ 27) $-8x^5y^3$

Multiplying a Polynomial and a Monomial

1) $x^2 + 3x$
2) $-8x + 16$
3) $4x^2 + 2x$
4) $-x^2 + 3x$
5) $9x^2 - 6x$
6) $15x - 30y$
7) $56x^2 - 32x$
8) $27x^2 + 6xy$
9) $6x^2 + 12xy$
10) $18x^2 + 36xy$
11) $36x^2 + 108x$
12) $22x^2 - 121xy$
13) $12x^2 - 12xy$
14) $6x^2 - 12xy + 6x$
15) $15x^3 + 10xy^2$
16) $52x^2 + 104xy$

17) $10x^2 - 45y^2$
18) $-6x^3y + 9xy$
19) $-4x^2 + 4xy - 4$
20) $3x^2 - 12xy - 24$
21) $4x^3 - 6x^2y + 4x^2$
22) $x^3 + 5x^2 - 4x^2y$
23) $9x^2 + 9xy - 72y^2$
24) $6x^3 - 9x^2 + 24x$
25) $40x^2 - 160x - 100$
26) $-x^4 + 3x^3 + 7x^2$
27) $x^5 - 2x^4 + 12x^3$
28) $18x^5 - 12x^4 + 12x^3$
29) $24x^4 - 40x^3y + 56x^2y^2$
30) $6x^4 - 10x^3 + 24x^2$
31) $4x^5 + 10x^4 - 8x^3$
32) $30x^3 - 25x^2y + 10xy^2$

Multiplying Binomials

1) $x^2 + 4x + 4$
2) $x^2 - x - 6$
3) $x^2 - 6x + 8$
4) $x^2 + 5x + 6$
5) $x^2 - 9x + 20$
6) $x^2 + 7x + 10$
7) $x^2 - 3x - 18$
8) $x^2 - 12x + 32$
9) $x^2 + 10x + 16$
10) $x^2 + 2x - 8$
11) $x^2 + 8x + 6$
12) $x^2 + 10x + 25$
13) $x^2 - 9$
14) $x^2 - 4$
15) $x^2 + 6x + 9$
16) $x^2 + 10x + 24$

17) $x^2 - 49$
18) $x^2 - 5x - 14$
19) $2x^2 + 8x + 6$
20) $4x^2 + 2x - 12$
21) $2x^2 - 8x - 64$
22) $x^2 - 13x + 42$
23) $x^2 - 64$
24) $12x^2 - 2x - 4$
25) $2x^2 + 9x - 35$
26) $15x^2 + 3x - 12$
27) $24x^2 + 90x + 81$
28) $10x^2 - 18x - 36$
29) $4x^2 + 8x - 32$
30) $36x^2 - 16$
31) $9x^2 - 3x - 12$
32) $x^4 - 4$

Factoring Trinomials

1) $(x + 3)(x + 5)$

2) $(x - 2)(x - 3)$

3) $(x + 4)(x + 2)$

4) $(x - 2)(x - 4)$

5) $(x - 4)(x - 4)$

6) $(x - 3)(x - 4)$

7) $(x + 2)(x + 9)$

8) $(x + 6)(x - 4)$

9) $(x - 2)(x + 6)$

10) $(x - 1)(x - 9)$

11) $(x - 2)(x + 7)$

12) $(x - 9)(x + 3)$

13) $(x + 3)(x - 14)$

14) $(x + 11)(x + 11)$

15) $(2x + 3)(3x - 4)$

16) $(x - 15)(x - 2)$

17) $(3x - 1)(x + 4)$

18) $(5x - 1)(2x + 7)$

19) $(x + 12)(x + 12)$

20) $(4x - 1)(2x + 3)$

21) $(x + 6)$

22) $(4x - 3)$

23) $(3x + 2)$

Operations with Polynomials

1) $54x + 18$

2) $24x + 56$

3) $30x - 5$

4) $-24x + 9$

5) $18x^3 - 15x^2$

6) $35x^3 - 10x^2$

7) $-18x^4 + 24x^3$

8) $-14x^5 + 28x^4$

9) $8x^2 + 16x - 24$

10) $16x^2 - 8x + 4$

11) $6x^2 + 4x - 4$

12) $40x^3 + 24x^2 + 64x$

13) $27x^2 - 6x - 1$

14) $24x^2 + 10x - 25$

15) $35x^2 + 27x - 18$

16) $9x^2 + 12x - 32$

17) $(5x + 4y)$

18) $8x^2 + 2x - 10$

19) $36x^2 + 108x + 81$

20) $34x$

21) $x^3 + 6x^2 + 12x + 6$

22) $(6x + 3y)$

Chapter 8: Functions Operations

Topics that you'll practice in this chapter:

- ✓ Evaluating Function
- ✓ Adding and Subtracting Functions
- ✓ Multiplying and Dividing Functions
- ✓ Composition of Functions

Mathematics is like checkers in being suitable for the young, not too difficult, amusing, and without peril to the state. — Plato

Evaluating Function

✍ *Write each of following in function notation.*

1) $h = 2x + 5$

2) $k = 12a - 9$

3) $d = 22t$

4) $y = 2x - 6$

5) $m = 25n - 120$

6) $c = p^2 + 5p + 5$

✍ *Evaluate each function.*

7) $f(x) = x - 2$, find $f(1)$

8) $g(x) = 2x + 3$, find $f(2)$

9) $h(x) = x + 8$, find $f(5)$

10) $f(x) = -x + 5$, find $f(4)$

11) $f(a) = 3a - 3$, find $f(-1)$

12) $h(x) = 12 - 2x$, find $f(6)$

13) $g(n) = 4n - 2$, find $f(-2)$

14) $f(x) = -5x + 3$, find $f(3)$

15) $k(n) = -8 + 4n$, find $f(2)$

16) $f(x) = -7x + 4$, find $f(-3)$

17) $g(n) = 10n - 3$, find $g(6)$

18) $g(n) = 8n + 4$, find $g(1)$

19) $h(x) = 4x - 22$, find $h(2)$

20) $h(n) = n^2 + 2$, find $h(3)$

21) $h(n) = n^2 - 7$, find $h(2)$

22) $h(n) = n^2 + 4$, find $h(-4)$

23) $h(n) = n^2 - 10$, find $h(5)$

24) $h(n) = -2n^2 - 6n$, find $h(2)$

25) $g(n) = 3n^2 + 2n$, find $g(2)$

26) $h(a) = -11a + 5$, find $h(2a)$

27) $k(a) = 7a + 3$, find $k(a - 2)$

28) $h(x) = 3x + 5$, find $h(6x)$

29) $h(x) = x^2 + 1$, find $h(\frac{x}{4})$

30) $h(x) = x^3 + 8$, find $h(3x)$

Adding and Subtracting Functions

✎ *Perform the indicated operation.*

1) $f(x) = 2x + 4$
   $g(x) = x + 3$
   Find $(f - g)(1)$

2) $g(a) = 2a - 1$
   $f(a) = -a - 4$
   Find $(g - f)(-1)$

3) $h(t) = 2t + 1$
   $g(t) = 2t + 2$
   Find $(h - g)(t)$

4) $g(a) = -3a - 3$
   $f(a) = a^2 + 5$
   Find $(g - f)(a)$

5) $g(x) = 2x - 5$
   $h(x) = 4x + 5$
   Find $g(3) - h(3)$

6) $h(3) = 3x + 3$
   $g(x) = -4x + 1$
   Find $(h + g)(10)$

7) $f(x) = 4x - 3$
   $g(x) = x^3 + 2x$
   Find $(f - g)(4)$

8) $h(n) = 4n + 5$
   $g(n) = 3n + 4$
   Find $(h - g)(n)$

9) $g(x) = -x^2 - 1 - 2x$
   $f(x) = 5 + x$
   Find $(g - f)(x)$

10) $g(t) = 2t + 5$
    $f(t) = -t^2 + 5$
    Find $(g + f)(t)$

11) $f(x) = 3x + 2$
    $g(x) = -2x^2 + x$
    Find $(f + g)(x)$

12) $f(x) = -2x^2 - 4x$
    $g(x) = 4x + 3$
    Find $(f + g)(x^2)$

Multiplying and Dividing Functions

✎ *Perform the indicated operation.*

1) $g(x) = -x - 2$

    $f(x) = 2x + 1$

    Find $(g.f)(2)$

2) $f(x) = 3x$

    $h(x) = -2x + 5$

    Find $(f.h)(-1)$

3) $g(a) = 2a - 1$

    $h(a) = 3a - 3$

    Find $(g.h)(-4)$

4) $f(x) = x + 4$

    $h(x) = 5x - 2$

    Find $\left(\frac{f}{h}\right)(2)$

5) $f(x) = 2a^2$

    $g(x) = -5 + 3a$

    Find $\left(\frac{f}{g}\right)(2)$

6) $g(a) = 3a + 2$

    $f(a) = 2a - 4$

    Find $\left(\frac{g}{f}\right)(3)$

7) $g(t) = t^2 + 3$

    $h(t) = 4t - 3$

    Find $(g.h)(-1)$

8) $g(n) = n^2 + 4 + 2n$

    $h(n) = -3n + 2$

    Find $(g.h)(1)$

9) $g(a) = 2a^3 - 5a + 2$

    $f(a) = a^3 - 4$

    Find $\left(\frac{g}{f}\right)(2)$

10) $g(x) = -2x^2 + 14 - 2x$

    $f(x) = x^2 + 5$

    Find $(g.f)(4)$

11) $f(x) = 2x^3 - 5x^2$

    $g(x) = 2x - 1$

    Find $(f.g)(x)$

12) $f(x) = 3x - 1$

    $g(x) = x^2 - x$

    Find $\left(\frac{f}{g}\right)(x)$

Composition of Functions

✎ **Using** f(x) = x + 2 **and** g(x) = 4x, **find:**

1) $f\big(g(1)\big) =$

2) $f\big(g(-2)\big) =$

3) $g\big(f(-1)\big) =$

4) $g\big(f(3)\big) =$

5) $f\big(g(2)\big) =$

6) $g\big(f(5)\big) =$

✎ **Using** f(x) = 5x + 4 **and** g(x) = x − 3, **find:**

7) $g\big(f(-3)\big) =$

8) $g\big(f(4)\big) =$

9) $f\big(g(6)\big) =$

10) $f\big(f(8)\big) =$

11) $g\big(f(-7)\big) =$

12) $g\big(f(x)\big) =$

✎ **Using** f(x) = 6x + 2 **and** g(x) = x − 5, **find:**

13) $g\big(f(-2)\big) =$

14) $f\big(f(4)\big) =$

15) $f\big(g(7)\big) =$

16) $f\big(f(2)\big) =$

17) $g\big(f(3)\big) =$

18) $g\big(g(x)\big) =$

✎ **Using** f(x) = 7x + 4 **and** g(x) = 2x − 4, **find:**

19) $f\big(g(-3)\big) =$

20) $g\big(f(-2)\big) =$

21) $f\big(g(3)\big) =$

22) $f\big(f(3)\big) =$

23) $g\big(f(4)\big) =$

24) $g\big(g(5)\big) =$

Answers of Worksheets – Chapter 8

Evaluating Function

1) $h(x) = 2x + 5$
2) $k(a) = 12a - 9$
3) $d(t) = 22t$
4) $f(x) = 2x - 6$
5) $m(n) = 25n - 120$
6) $c(p) = p^2 + 5p + 5$
7) -1
8) 7
9) 13
10) 1
11) -6

12) 0
13) -10
14) -12
15) 0
16) 25
17) 57
18) 12
19) -14
20) 11
21) -3
22) 20

23) 15
24) -20
25) 16
26) $-22a + 5$
27) $7a - 11$
28) $18x + 5$
29) $\frac{1}{16}x^2 + 1$
30) $27x^3 + 8$

Adding and Subtracting Functions

1) 2
2) 0
3) -1
4) $-a^2 - 3a - 8$
5) -16
6) -6

7) -59
8) $n + 1$
9) $-x^2 - 3x - 6$
10) $-t^2 + 2t + 10$
11) $-2x^2 + 4x + 2$
12) $-2x^6 + 3$

Multiplying and Dividing Functions

1) -20
2) -21
3) 135
4) $\frac{6}{8} = \frac{3}{4}$
5) 8
6) $\frac{11}{2}$

7) -28
8) -7
9) 2
10) -546
11) $4x^4 - 12x^3 + 5x^2$
12) $\frac{3x-1}{x^2-x}$

Composition of Functions

1) 6

2) −6

3) 4

4) 20

5) 10

6) 28

7) −14

8) 24

9) 19

10) 41

11) −31

12) $5x + 1$

13) −15

14) 21

15) 14

16) 86

17) 15

18) $x − 10$

19) −66

20) −24

21) 18

22) 179

23) 60

24) 8

Chapter 9: Logarithms

Topics that you'll practice in this chapter:

- ✓ Rewriting Logarithms
- ✓ Evaluating Logarithms
- ✓ Properties of Logarithms
- ✓ Natural Logarithms
- ✓ Exponential Equations Requiring Logarithms
- ✓ Solving Logarithmic Equations

Mathematics is an art of human understanding. — William Thurston

Rewriting Logarithms

 Rewrite each equation in exponential form.

1) $\log_5 25 = 2$

2) $\log_4 256 = 4$

3) $\log_6 36 = 2$

4) $\log_5 125 = 3$

5) $\log_7 49 = 2$

6) $\log_6 216 = 3$

7) $\log_2 16 = 4$

8) $\log_3 81 = 4$

9) $\log_{10} 100 = 2$

10) $\log_7 343 = 3$

11) $\log_4 64 = 3$

12) $\log_9 81 = 2$

13) $\log_5 625 = 4$

14) $\log_9 3 = \frac{1}{2}$

15) $\log_{64} 8 = \frac{1}{2}$

16) $\log_{125} 5 = \frac{1}{3}$

17) $\log_{16} 2 = \frac{1}{4}$

18) $\log_8 \frac{1}{64} = -2$

19) $\log_5 \frac{1}{125} = -3$

20) $\log_a \frac{5}{8} = b$

Rewrite each exponential equation in logarithmic form.

21) $3^4 = 81$

22) $5^2 = 25$

23) $2^5 = 32$

24) $6^3 = 216$

25) $7^2 = 49$

26) $8^3 = 512$

27) $5^3 = 125$

28) $2^8 = 256$

29) $2^{-3} = \frac{1}{8}$

30) $3^{-4} = \frac{1}{81}$

31) $5^{-2} = \frac{1}{25}$

32) $6^{-3} = \frac{1}{216}$

33) $4^{-3} = \frac{1}{64}$

34) $2^{-6} = \frac{1}{64}$

Evaluating Logarithms

✍ *Evaluate each logarithm.*

1) $\log_2 4 =$

2) $\log_2 8 =$

3) $\log_3 27 =$

4) $\log_3 9 =$

5) $\log_4 16 =$

6) $\log_2 32 =$

7) $\log_8 64 =$

8) $\log_2 \frac{1}{2} =$

9) $\log_2 \frac{1}{8} =$

10) $\log_3 \frac{1}{3} =$

11) $\log_4 \frac{1}{16} =$

12) $\log_3 \frac{1}{9} =$

13) $\log_7 \frac{1}{49} =$

14) $\log_{64} \frac{1}{4} =$

15) $\log_{625} 5 =$

16) $\log_2 \frac{1}{64} =$

17) $\log_4 \frac{1}{64} =$

18) $\log_{36} \frac{1}{6} =$

✍ *Circle the points which are on the graph of the given logarithmic functions.*

19) $y = 2\log_3(x+1) + 2$ $(2,4)$, $(8,4)$, $(0,3)$

20) $y = 3\log_3(3x) - 2$ $(3,6)$, $(3,4)$, $(\frac{1}{3},2)$

21) $y = -2\log_2 2(x-1) + 1$ $(3,-3)$, $(2,1)$, $(5,5)$

22) $y = 4\log_4(4x) + 7$ $(1,7)$, $(1,11)$, $(4,8)$

23) $y = -\log_2 2(x+3) + 1$ $(-2,0)$, $(1,2)$, $(5,3)$

24) $y = -\log_5(x-3) + 8$ $(4,8)$, $(8,8)$, $(4,4)$

25) $y = 3\log_4(x+1) + 3$ $(3,3)$, $(3,6)$, $(0,4)$

Properties of Logarithms

 Expand each logarithm.

1) $log\ (8 \times 5) =$

2) $log\ (9 \times 4) =$

3) $log\ (3 \times 7) =$

4) $log\ (\frac{3}{4}) =$

5) $log\ (\frac{5}{7}) =$

6) $log\ (\frac{2}{5})^3 =$

7) $log\ (2 \times 3^4) =$

8) $log\ (\frac{5}{7})^4 =$

9) $log\ \left(\frac{2^3}{7}\right) =$

10) $log\ (x \times y)^5 =$

11) $log\ (x^3 \times y \times z^4) =$

12) $log\ \left(\frac{u^4}{v}\right) =$

13) $log\ \left(\frac{x}{y^6}\right) =$

 Condense each expression to a single logarithm.

14) $log\ 2 - log\ 9 =$

15) $log\ 5 + log\ 3 =$

16) $5\ log\ 6 - 3\ log\ 4 =$

17) $4\ log\ 7 - 2\ log\ 9 =$

18) $3\ log\ 5 -\ log\ 14 =$

19) $7\ log\ 3 -\ 4log\ 4 =$

20) $log\ 7 - 2\ log\ 12 =$

21) $2log\ 5 + 3log\ 8 =$

22) $4log\ 3 + 5log\ 7 =$

23) $4\ log_5\ a + 7\ log_5\ b =$

24) $2log_3\ x - 9\ log_3\ y =$

25) $log_4\ u - 6\ log_4\ v =$

26) $4\ log_6\ u + 8\ log_6\ v =$

27) $4\ log_3\ u - 20\ log_3\ v =$

Natural Logarithms

✍ *Solve each equation for* x.

1) $e^x = 3$

2) $e^x = 4$

3) $e^x = 8$

4) $\ln x = 6$

5) $\ln(\ln x) = 5$

6) $e^x = 9$

7) $\ln(2x + 5) = 4$

8) $\ln(2x - 1) = 1$

9) $\ln(6x - 1) = 1$

10) $\ln x = \frac{1}{2}$

11) $\ln 2x = e^2$

12) $\ln x = \ln 4 + \ln 7$

13) $\ln x = 2\ln 4 + \ln 5$

✍ *Evaluate without using a calculator.*

14) $\ln 1 =$

15) $\ln e^3 =$

16) $2 \ln e =$

17) $\ln e^2 =$

18) $4\ln e =$

19) $\ln\left(\frac{1}{e}\right) =$

20) $e^{\ln 10} =$

21) $e^{3\ln 2} =$

22) $e^{5\ln 2} =$

23) $\ln \sqrt{e} =$

✍ *Reduce the following expressions to simplest form.*

24) $e^{-2\ln 5 + 2\ln 3} =$

25) $e^{-\ln\left(\frac{1}{e}\right)} =$

26) $2 \ln(e^3) =$

27) $\ln\left(\frac{1}{e}\right)^2 =$

28) $e^{\ln 2 + 3\ln 2} =$

29) $e^{\ln\left(\frac{2}{e}\right)} =$

30) $5 \ln(1^{-e}) =$

31) $\ln\left(\frac{1}{e}\right)^{-3} =$

32) $\ln\left(\frac{\sqrt{e}}{e}\right) =$

33) $e^{-2\ln e + 2\ln 2} =$

34) $e^{\ln\frac{1}{e}} =$

35) $3 \ln(e^e) =$

Exponential Equations and Logarithms

 Solve each equation for the unknown variable.

1) $5^{3n} = 125$

2) $3^r = 69$

3) $20^n = 56$

4) $4^{r+1} = 1$

5) $243^x = 81$

6) $6^{-3v-2} = 36$

7) $3^{2n} = 9$

8) $6^n = 51$

9) $\frac{216^{2a}}{36^{-a}} = 216$

10) $25 \times 25^{-v} = 625$

11) $3^{2n} = \frac{1}{81}$

12) $(\frac{1}{6})^n = 36$

13) $32^{2x} = 8$

14) $5^{3-2x} = 5^{-x}$

15) $2^{-3x} = 2^{x-1}$

16) $2^{2n} = 16$

17) $2^{2x+2} = 2^{3x}$

18) $5^{3n} = 125$

19) $3^{-2k} = 81$

20) $5^{3r} = 5^{-2r}$

21) $4^{-2r} \times 4^r = 64$

22) $10^{3x} = 10,000$

23) $25 \cdot 125^{-v} = 625$

24) $\frac{125}{25^{-3m}} = 25^{-2m-2}$

25) $2^{-2n} \times 2^{n+1} = 2^{-2n}$

26) $6^{3n} \times 6^{-n} = 6^{-2n}$

 Solve each problem. (Round to the nearest whole number)

27) A substance decays 18% each day. After 12 days, there are 6 milligrams of the substance remaining. How many milligrams were there initially? _____

28) A culture of bacteria grows continuously. The culture doubles every 3 hours. If the initial amount of bacteria is 10, how many bacteria will there be in 13 hours? _____

29) Bob plans to invest $5,500 at an annual rate of 4.5%. How much will Bob have in the account after five years if the balance is compounded quarterly? _____

30) Suppose you plan to invest $4,000 at an annual rate of 5.5%. How much will you have in the account after 10 years if the balance is compounded monthly? _____

Solving Logarithmic Equations

 Find the value of the variables in each equation.

1) $2\log_7 - 2x = 0$

2) $-\log_5 7x = 2$

3) $\log x + 5 = 2$

4) $\log x - \log 4 = 3$

5) $\log x + \log 2 = 4$

6) $\log 10 + \log x = 1$

7) $\log x + \log 8 = \log 48$

8) $-3\log_3(x - 2) = -12$

9) $\log 6x = \log (x + 5)$

10) $\log (4k - 5) = \log (2k - 1)$

11) $\log(4p - 2) = \log(-5p + 5)$

12) $-10 + \log_3 (n + 3) = -10$

13) $\log_9(x + 2) = \log_9 (x^2 + 30)$

14) $\log_{12} (v^2 + 35) = \log_{12} (-2v - 1)$

15) $\log (16 + 2b) = \log (b^2 - 4b)$

16) $\log_9(x + 6) - \log_9 x = \log_9 2$

17) $\log_5 6 + \log_5 2x^2 = \log_5 48$

18) $\log_6(x + 1) - \log_6 x = \log_6 29$

Find the value of x *in each natural logarithm equation.*

19) $\ln 2 - \ln(3x + 2) = 1$

20) $\ln(x - 3) - \ln(x - 5) = \ln 5$

21) $\ln e^4 - \ln(x + 1) = 1$

22) $\ln(2x - 1) - \ln(x - 5) = \ln 5$

23) $\ln 2x + \ln(3x - 4) = \ln 4x$

24) $\ln(4x - 2) - 4\ln(x - 5) = \ln 10$

25) $\ln(4x + 2) - \ln 1 = 5$

26) $\ln(x - 3) + \ln(x - 5) = \ln 2$

27) $\ln 2 + \ln(3x + 2) = 4$

28) $2 \ln 4x - \ln(x + 6) = 2 \ln 3x$

29) $\ln x^2 + \ln x^3 = \ln 1$

30) $\ln x^4 - \ln(x + 4) = 4 \ln x$

31) $2 \ln(x - 3) = \ln(x^2 - 6x + 9)$

32) $\ln(x^2 + 12) = \ln(6x + 4)$

33) $2 \ln x - 2\ln(x + 2) = 4\ln(x^2)$

34) $\ln(4x - 3) - \ln(2x - 4) = \ln 5$

35) $\ln 2 + 4 \ln(x + 2) = \ln 2$

36) $2\ln e^2 + \ln(2x - 1) = \ln 5 + 4$

Answers of Worksheets – Chapter 9

Rewriting Logarithms

1) $5^2 = 25$
2) $4^4 = 256$
3) $6^2 = 36$
4) $5^3 = 125$
5) $7^2 = 49$
6) $6^3 = 216$
7) $2^4 = 16$
8) $3^4 = 81$
9) $10^2 = 100$
10) $7^3 = 343$
11) $4^3 = 64$
12) $9^2 = 81$
13) $5^4 = 625$
14) $9^{\frac{1}{2}} = 3$
15) $64^{\frac{1}{2}} = 8$

16) $125^{\frac{1}{3}} = 5$
17) $16^{\frac{1}{4}} = 2$
18) $8^{-2} = \frac{1}{64}$
19) $5^{-3} = \frac{1}{125}$
20) $a^b = \frac{5}{8}$
21) $log_3 81 = 4$
22) $log_5 25 = 2$
23) $log_2 32 = 5$
24) $log_6 216 = 3$
25) $log_7 49 = 2$
26) $log_8 512 = 3$

27) $log_5 125 = 3$
28) $log_2 256 = 8$
29) $log_2 \frac{1}{8} = -3$
30) $log_3 \frac{1}{81} = -4$
31) $log_5 \frac{1}{25} = -2$
32) $log_6 \frac{1}{216} = -3$
33) $log_4 \frac{1}{64} = -3$
34) $log_2 \frac{1}{64} = -6$

Evaluating Logarithms

1) 2
2) 3
3) 3
4) 2
5) 2
6) 5
7) 2
8) -1
9) -3

10) -1
11) -2
12) -2
13) -2
14) $-\frac{1}{3}$
15) -4
16) -6
17) -3

18) $-\frac{1}{2}$
19) $(2, 4)$
20) $(3, 4)$
21) $(3, -3)$
22) $(1, 11)$
23) $(-2, 1)$
24) $(4, 8)$
25) $(3, 6)$

Properties of Logarithms

1) $log\, 8 + log\, 5$
2) $log\, 9 + log\, 9$
3) $log\, 3 + log\, 7$
4) $log\, 3 - log\, 4$
5) $log\, 5 - log\, 7$
6) $3\, log\, 2 - 3\, log\, 5$

7) $log\, 2 + 4\, log\, 3$
8) $4log\, 5 - 4\, log\, 7$
9) $3\, log\, 2 - log\, 7$
10) $5\, log\, x + 5\, log\, y$
11) $log\, x + log\, y + 4\, log\, z$
12) $4\, log\, u - log\, v$

13) $\log x - 6 \log y$

14) $\log \frac{2}{9}$

15) $\log(5 \cdot 3)$

16) $\log \frac{6^5}{4^3}$

17) $\log \frac{7^4}{9^2}$

18) $\log \frac{5^3}{14}$

19) $\log \frac{3^7}{4^4}$

20) $\log \frac{7}{12^2}$

21) $\log (5^2 8^3)$

22) $\log (3^4 7^5)$

23) $\log_5 (a^4 b^7)$

24) $\log_3 \frac{x^2}{y^9}$

25) $\log_4 \frac{u}{v^6}$

26) $\log_6 (u^4 \times v^8)$

27) $\log_3 \frac{u^4}{v^{20}}$

Natural Logarithms

1) $x = \ln 3$

2) $x = \ln 4, x = 2\ln(2)$

3) $x = \ln 8, x = 3\ln(2)$

4) $x = e^6$

5) $x = e^{e^5}$

6) $x = \ln 9, x = 2\ln(3)$

7) $x = \frac{e^4 - 5}{2}$

8) $x = \frac{e+1}{2}$

9) $x = \frac{e+1}{6}$

10) $x = \sqrt{e}$

11) $x = \frac{e e^2}{2}$

12) $x = 28$

13) $x = 80$

14)   0

15)   3

16)   2

17)   2

18)   4

19) -1

20)   10

21)   8

22) 32

23) $\frac{1}{2}$

24) $\frac{9}{25} = 0.36$

25) e

26) 6

27) -2

28) 16

29) $\frac{2}{e}$

30) 0

31) 3

32) -0.5

33) $4e^{-2} = \frac{4}{e^2}$

34) $\frac{1}{e}$

35) $3e$

Exponential Equations and Logarithms

1) 1

2) 3.854

3) 1.3437

4) -1

5) $\frac{4}{5}$

6) $-\frac{4}{3}$

7) 1

8) 51

9) $\frac{3}{8}$

10) -1

11) -2

12) -2

13) $\frac{3}{10}$

14) 3

15) $\frac{1}{4}$

16)   2

17)   2

18)   1

19) -2

20) 0

21) -3

22) $\frac{4}{3}$

23) -1

24) $-\frac{7}{10}$

25) -1

26) 0

27) 52

28) 202

29) $6879.13

30) $6,924.31

Solving Logarithmic Equations

1) $\{-\frac{1}{2}\}$

2) $\{\frac{1}{175}\}$

3) $\{-\frac{1}{1,000}\}$

4) $\{4,000\}$

5) $\{5,000\}$

6) $\{1\}$

7) $\{6\}$

8) $\{83\}$

9) $\{1\}$

10) $\{2\}$

11) $\{\frac{7}{9}\}$

12) $\{-2\}$

13) No Solution

14) No Solution

15) $\{8, -2\}$

16) $\{6\}$

17) $\{\sqrt{3}, -\sqrt{3}\}$

18) $\{\frac{1}{28}\}$

19) $x = \frac{2-2e}{3e} = -0.42$

20) $\{\frac{11}{2}\}$

21) $e^3 - 1$

22) $\{8\}$

23) $\{2\}$

24) $\{6.23\}$

25) $x = \frac{e^5-2}{4}$

26) $x = 4 + \sqrt{3}$

27) $x = \frac{e^4-4}{6}$

28) No Solution

29) $\{1\}$

30) No Solution

31) $x > 3$

32) $\{2, 4\}$

33) $\{0.71667 \dots\}$

34) $\{\frac{17}{6}\}$

35) $\{-1\}$

36) $\{3\}$

Chapter 10: Radical Expressions

Topics that you'll practice in this chapter:

- ✓ Simplifying Radical Expressions
- ✓ Simplifying Radical Expressions Involving Fractions
- ✓ Multiplying Radical Expressions
- ✓ Adding and Subtracting Radical Expressions
- ✓ Domain and Range of Radical Functions
- ✓ Solving Radical Equations

Mathematics is an independent world created out of pure intelligence.

— William Woods Worth

Simplifying Radical Expressions

✍ **Simplify.**

1) $\sqrt{35x^2} =$

2) $\sqrt{90x^2} =$

3) $\sqrt[3]{8a} =$

4) $\sqrt{100x^3} =$

5) $\sqrt{125a} =$

6) $\sqrt[3]{88w^3} =$

7) $\sqrt{80x} =$

8) $\sqrt{216v} =$

9) $\sqrt[3]{125x}$

10) $\sqrt{64x^5} =$

11) $\sqrt{4x^2} =$

12) $\sqrt[3]{54a^2}$

13) $\sqrt{405} =$

14) $\sqrt{512p^3} =$

15) $\sqrt{216m^4} =$

16) $\sqrt{264x^3y^3} =$

17) $\sqrt{49x^3y^3} =$

18) $\sqrt{16a^4b^3} =$

19) $\sqrt{20x^3y^3} =$

20) $\sqrt[3]{216yx^3} =$

21) $3\sqrt{75x^2} =$

22) $5\sqrt{80x^2} =$

23) $\sqrt[3]{256x^2y^3} =$

24) $\sqrt[3]{343x^4y^2} =$

25) $4\sqrt{125a} =$

26) $\sqrt[3]{625xy} =$

27) $2\sqrt{8x^2y^3r} =$

28) $4\sqrt{36x^2y^3z^4} =$

29) $2\sqrt[3]{512x^3y^4} =$

30) $5\sqrt{64a^2b^3c^5} =$

31) $2\sqrt[3]{125x^6y^{12}} =$

Multiplying Radical Expressions

✎ **Simplify.**

1) $\sqrt{5} \times \sqrt{5} =$

2) $\sqrt{5} \times \sqrt{10} =$

3) $\sqrt{2} \times \sqrt{18} =$

4) $\sqrt{14} \times \sqrt{21} =$

5) $\sqrt{5} \times -4\sqrt{20} =$

6) $3\sqrt{12} \times \sqrt{6} =$

7) $5\sqrt{42} \times \sqrt{3} =$

8) $\sqrt{3} \times -\sqrt{25} =$

9) $\sqrt{99} \times \sqrt{48} =$

10) $5\sqrt{45} \times 3\sqrt{176} =$

11) $\sqrt{12}(3 + \sqrt{3}) =$

12) $\sqrt{23x^2} \times \sqrt{23x} =$

13) $-5\sqrt{12} \times -\sqrt{3} =$

14) $2\sqrt{20x^2} \times \sqrt{5x^2} =$

15) $\sqrt{12x^2} \times \sqrt{2x^3} =$

16) $-12\sqrt{7x} \times \sqrt{5x^3} =$

17) $-5\sqrt{9x^3} \times 6\sqrt{3x^2} =$

18) $-2\sqrt{12}(3 + \sqrt{12}) =$

19) $\sqrt{18x}(4 - \sqrt{6x}) =$

20) $\sqrt{3x}(6\sqrt{x^3} + \sqrt{27}) =$

21) $\sqrt{15r}(5 + \sqrt{5}) =$

22) $-5\sqrt{3x} \times 4\sqrt{6x^3} =$

23) $-2\sqrt{18x} \times 4\sqrt{2x}$

24) $-3\sqrt{5v^2}(-3\sqrt{15v}) =$

25) $(\sqrt{5} - \sqrt{3})(\sqrt{5} + \sqrt{3}) =$

26) $(-4\sqrt{6} + 2)(\sqrt{6} - 5) =$

27) $(2 - 2\sqrt{3})(-2 + \sqrt{3}) =$

28) $(11 - 4\sqrt{5})(6 - \sqrt{5}) =$

29) $(-2 - \sqrt{3x})(3 + \sqrt{3x}) =$

30) $(-2 + 3\sqrt{2r})(-2 + \sqrt{2r}) =$

31) $(-4\sqrt{2n} + 2)(-2\sqrt{2} - 4) =$

32) $(-1 + 2\sqrt{3})(2 - 3\sqrt{3x}) =$

Simplifying Radical Expressions Involving Fractions

✑ **Simplify.**

1) $\dfrac{\sqrt{5}}{\sqrt{3}} =$

2) $\dfrac{\sqrt{8}}{\sqrt{100}} =$

3) $\dfrac{\sqrt{2}}{2\sqrt{3}} =$

4) $\dfrac{4}{\sqrt{5}} =$

5) $\dfrac{2\sqrt{5r}}{\sqrt{m^3}} =$

6) $\dfrac{8\sqrt{3}}{\sqrt{k}} =$

7) $\dfrac{6\sqrt{14x^2}}{2\sqrt{18x}} =$

8) $\dfrac{\sqrt{7x^2y^2}}{\sqrt{5x^3y^2}} =$

9) $\dfrac{1}{1+\sqrt{2}} =$

10) $\dfrac{1-5\sqrt{a}}{\sqrt{11a}} =$

11) $\dfrac{\sqrt{a}}{\sqrt{a}+\sqrt{b}} =$

12) $\dfrac{1+\sqrt{2}}{3+\sqrt{5}} =$

13) $\dfrac{2+\sqrt{5}}{6-\sqrt{3}} =$

14) $\dfrac{5}{-3-3\sqrt{3}}$

15) $\dfrac{2}{3+\sqrt{5}} =$

16) $\dfrac{\sqrt{7}-\sqrt{3}}{\sqrt{3}-\sqrt{7}} =$

17) $\dfrac{\sqrt{7}+\sqrt{5}}{\sqrt{5}+\sqrt{2}} =$

18) $\dfrac{3\sqrt{2}-\sqrt{7}}{4\sqrt{2}+\sqrt{5}} =$

19) $\dfrac{\sqrt{5}+2\sqrt{2}}{4-\sqrt{5}} =$

20) $\dfrac{5\sqrt{3}-3\sqrt{2}}{3\sqrt{2}-2\sqrt{3}} =$

21) $\dfrac{\sqrt{8a^5b^3}}{\sqrt{2ab^2}} =$

22) $\dfrac{6\sqrt{45\ ^3}}{3\sqrt{5x}} =$

Adding and Subtracting Radical Expressions

✎ *Simplify.*

1) $\sqrt{3} + \sqrt{27} =$

2) $3\sqrt{8} + 3\sqrt{2} =$

3) $4\sqrt{3} - 2\sqrt{12} =$

4) $3\sqrt{18} - 2\sqrt{2} =$

5) $2\sqrt{45} - 2\sqrt{5} =$

6) $-\sqrt{12} - 5\sqrt{3} =$

7) $-4\sqrt{2} - 5\sqrt{32} =$

8) $5\sqrt{10} + 2\sqrt{40} =$

9) $4\sqrt{12} - 3\sqrt{27} =$

10) $-3\sqrt{2} + 4\sqrt{18} =$

11) $-10\sqrt{7} + 6\sqrt{28} =$

12) $5\sqrt{3} - \sqrt{27} =$

13) $-\sqrt{12} + 3\sqrt{3} =$

14) $-3\sqrt{6} - \sqrt{54} =$

15) $3\sqrt{8} + 3\sqrt{2} =$

16) $2\sqrt{12} - 3\sqrt{27} =$

17) $\sqrt{50} - \sqrt{32} =$

18) $4\sqrt{8} - 6\sqrt{2} =$

19) $-4\sqrt{12} + 12\sqrt{108} =$

20) $2\sqrt{45} - 2\sqrt{5} =$

21) $7\sqrt{18} - 3\sqrt{2} =$

22) $-12\sqrt{35} + 7\sqrt{140} =$

23) $-6\sqrt{19} - 3\sqrt{76} =$

24) $-\sqrt{54x} - 3\sqrt{6x} =$

25) $\sqrt{5y^2} + y\sqrt{45} =$

26) $\sqrt{8mn^2} + 2n\sqrt{18m} =$

27) $-8\sqrt{27a} - 5\sqrt{3a} =$

28) $-4\sqrt{7ab} - \sqrt{28ab} =$

29) $\sqrt{27a^2b} + a\sqrt{12b} =$

30) $3\sqrt{6a^3} - 2\sqrt{24a^3} + 2a\sqrt{54a} =$

Domain and Range of Radical Functions

✍ *Identify the domain and range of each function.*

1) $y = \sqrt{x+2} - 3$

2) $y = \sqrt[3]{x-1} - 1$

3) $y = \sqrt{x-2} + 5$

4) $y = \sqrt[3]{(x+1)} - 4$

5) $y = 3\sqrt{3x+6} + 5$

6) $y = \sqrt[3]{(2x-1)} - 4$

7) $y = 6\sqrt{3x^2+6} + 5$

8) $y = \sqrt[3]{(2x^2 - 2)} - 4$

9) $y = 4\sqrt{4x^3 + 32} - 1$

10) $y = \sqrt[3]{(4x+8)} - 2x$

11) $y = 7\sqrt{-2(2x+4)} + 1$

12) $y = \sqrt[5]{(4x^2 - 5)} - 2$

13) $y = 2x\sqrt{5x^4 + 6} - 2x$

14) $y = 6\sqrt[3]{(8x^6 + 2x + 8)} - 2$

✍ *Sketch the graph of each function.*

10) $y = \sqrt{x} + 8$

11) $y = 2\sqrt{x} - 4$

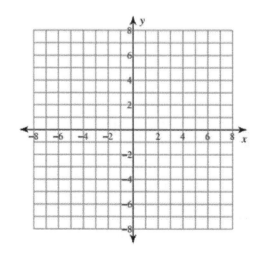

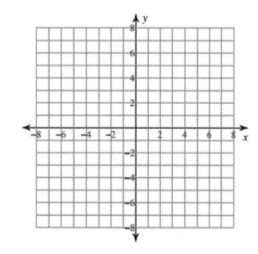

Solving Radical Equations

✍ **Solve each equation. Remember to check for extraneous solutions.**

1) $\sqrt{a} = 5$

2) $\sqrt{v} = 3$

3) $\sqrt{r} = 4$

4) $2 = 4\sqrt{x}$

5) $\sqrt{x+1} = 9$

6) $1 = \sqrt{x-5}$

7) $6 = \sqrt{r-2}$

8) $\sqrt{x-6} = 8$

9) $5 = \sqrt{x-3}$

10) $\sqrt{m+8} = 8$

11) $10\sqrt{9a} = 60$

12) $5\sqrt{3x} = 15$

13) $1 = \sqrt{3x-5}$

14) $\sqrt{12-x} = x$

15) $\sqrt{r+3} - 1 = 7$

16) $-12 = -6\sqrt{r+4}$

17) $20 = 2\sqrt{36v}$

18) $x = \sqrt{42-x}$

19) $\sqrt{110-a} = a$

20) $\sqrt{2n-12} = 2$

21) $\sqrt{3r-5} = r-3$

22) $\sqrt{-16+10x} = x$

23) $\sqrt{3x+12} = \sqrt{x+8}$

24) $\sqrt{v} = \sqrt{2v-6}$

25) $\sqrt{11-x} = \sqrt{x-7}$

26) $\sqrt{m+8} = \sqrt{3m+8}$

27) $\sqrt{2r+40} = \sqrt{-16-2r}$

28) $\sqrt{k+3} = \sqrt{1-k}$

29) $-10\sqrt{x-10} = -60$

30) $\sqrt{72-x} = \sqrt{\dfrac{x}{5}}$

Answers of Worksheets – Chapter 10

Simplifying radical expressions

1) $x\sqrt{35}$

2) $3x\sqrt{10}$

3) $2\sqrt[3]{a}$

4) $10x\sqrt{x}$

5) $5\sqrt{5a}$

6) $2w\sqrt[3]{11}$

7) $4\sqrt{5x}$

8) $6\sqrt{6v}$

9) $5\sqrt[3]{x}$

10) $8x^2\sqrt{x}$

11) $2x$

12) $3\sqrt[3]{2a^2}$

13) $9\sqrt{5}$

14) $16p\sqrt{2p}$

15) $6m^2\sqrt{6}$

16) $2x.\,y\sqrt{66xy}$

17) $7xy\sqrt{xy}$

18) $4a^2b\sqrt{b}$

19) $2xy\sqrt{5xy}$

20) $6x\sqrt[3]{y}$

21) $15x\sqrt{3}$

22) $20x\sqrt{5}$

23) $16y\sqrt[3]{x^2}$

24) $7x\sqrt[3]{xy^2}$

25) $20\sqrt{5a}$

26) $5\sqrt[3]{5xy}$

27) $4xy\sqrt{2yr}$

28) $24\,x\,yz^2\sqrt{y}$

29) $16xy\sqrt[3]{y}$

30) $40abc^2\sqrt{bc}$

31) $10x^2y^4$

Multiplying radical expressions

1) 5

2) $5\sqrt{2}$

3) 6

4) $7\sqrt{6}$

5) -40

6) $18\sqrt{2}$

7) $15\sqrt{14}$

8) $-5\sqrt{3}$

9) $12\sqrt{33}$

10) $180\sqrt{55}$

11) $6\sqrt{3}+6$

12) $23x\sqrt{x}$

13) 30

14) $20x^2$

15) $2x\sqrt{6x}$

16) $-12x^2\sqrt{35}$

17) $-90x^2\sqrt{3x}$

18) $-12\sqrt{3}-24$

19) $6\sqrt{2x}-6x\sqrt{3}$

20) $54x^2$

21) $5\sqrt{15r}+3\sqrt{5r}$

22) $-60x^2\sqrt{2}$

23) $-48x$

24) $45v\sqrt{3v}$

25) 2

26) $22\sqrt{3} - 34$

27) $6\sqrt{3} - 10$

28) $86 - 35\sqrt{5}$

29) $-3x - 5\sqrt{3x} - 6$

30) $12r - 8\sqrt{2r} + 4$

31) $16\sqrt{n} + 16\sqrt{2n} - 4\sqrt{2} - 8$

32) $-2 + 3\sqrt{3x} + 4\sqrt{3} - 18\sqrt{x}$

Simplifying radical expressions involving fractions

1) $\frac{\sqrt{15}}{3}$

2) $\frac{\sqrt{2}}{5}$

3) $\frac{\sqrt{6}}{6}$

4) $\frac{4\sqrt{5}}{5}$

5) $\frac{2\sqrt{5m}}{m^2}$

6) $\frac{8\sqrt{3k}}{k}$

7) $\sqrt{7x}$

8) $\frac{\sqrt{35x}}{5x}$

9) $-1 + \sqrt{2}$

10) $\frac{\sqrt{11} - 5a\sqrt{11}}{11a}$

11) $\frac{a - \sqrt{ab}}{a - b}$

12) $\frac{3 - \sqrt{5} + 3\sqrt{2} - \sqrt{10}}{4}$

13) $\frac{12 + 2\sqrt{3} + 6\sqrt{5} + \sqrt{15}}{33}$

14) $\frac{5 - 5\sqrt{5}}{6}$

15) $-3 + \sqrt{5}$

16) -1

17) $\frac{\sqrt{35} - \sqrt{14} + 5 - \sqrt{10}}{3}$

18) $\frac{24 - 3\sqrt{10} - 4\sqrt{14} + \sqrt{35}}{27}$

19) $\frac{4\sqrt{5} + 5 + 8\sqrt{2} + 2\sqrt{10}}{11}$

20) $\frac{3\sqrt{6} + 4}{2}$

21) $2a^2\sqrt{b}$

22) $6x$

Adding and subtracting radical expressions

1) $4\sqrt{3}$

2) $9\sqrt{2}$

3) 0

4) $7\sqrt{2}$

5) $4\sqrt{5}$

6) $-7\sqrt{3}$

7) $-24\sqrt{2}$

8) $9\sqrt{10}$

9) $-\sqrt{3}$

10) $9\sqrt{2}$

11) $2\sqrt{7}$

12) $2\sqrt{3}$

13) $\sqrt{3}$

14) 0

15) $9\sqrt{2}$

16) $-5\sqrt{3}$

17) $\sqrt{2}$

18) $2\sqrt{2}$

19) $64\sqrt{3}$

20) $4\sqrt{5}$

21) $18\sqrt{2}$

22) $2\sqrt{35}$

23) $-12\sqrt{19}$

24) $-6\sqrt{6x}$

25) $4y\sqrt{5}$

26) $8n\sqrt{2m}$

27) $-29\sqrt{3a}$

28) $-8\sqrt{7ab}$

29) $5a\sqrt{3b}$

30) $5a\sqrt{6a}$

Domain and range of radical functions

1) domain: $x \geq -2$

   range: $y \geq -3$

2) domain: {all real numbers}

   range: {all real numbers}

3) domain: $x \geq 2$

   range: $y \geq 5$

4) domain: {all real numbers}

   range: {all real numbers}

5) domain: $x \geq -2$

   range: $y \geq 5$

6) domain: {all real numbers}

   range: {all real numbers}

7) domain: {all real numbers}

   range: {all real numbers}

8) domain: {all real numbers}

   range: {all real numbers}

9) domain: $x \geq -2$

   range: $y \geq -1$

10) domain: {all real numbers}

    range: {all real numbers}

11) domain: $x \leq -2$

    range: $y \geq 1$

12) domain: {all real numbers}

    range: {all real numbers}

13) domain: {all real numbers}

    range: {all real numbers}

14) domain: {all real numbers}

    range: {all real numbers}

5)   6)

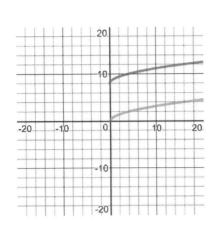   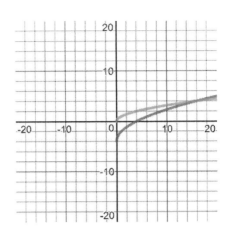

Solving radical equations

1) {25}

2) {9}

3) {16}

4) $\{\frac{1}{4}\}$

5) {80}

6) {6}

7) {38}

8) {70}

9) {28}

10) {56}

11) {4}

12) {3}

13) {2}

14) {3}

15) {61}

16) {0}

17) $\{\frac{25}{9}\}$

18) {6}

19) {10}

20) {8}

21) {4}

22) {2, 8}

23) {−2}

24) {6}

25) {9}

26) {0}

27) {−14}

28) {−1}

29) {46}

30) {60}

Chapter 11: Rational Expressions

Topics that you'll learn in this chapter:

- ✓ Simplifying and Graphing Rational Expressions
- ✓ Adding and Subtracting Rational Expressions
- ✓ Multiplying and Dividing Rational Expressions
- ✓ Solving Rational Equations and Complex Fractions

Simplifying and Graphing Rational Expressions

✎ **Simplify.**

1) $\dfrac{x+3}{3x+9} =$

2) $\dfrac{2x^2 - 2x - 12}{x-3} =$

3) $\dfrac{16}{4x-4} =$

4) $\dfrac{36x^3}{42x^3} =$

5) $\dfrac{x^2 - 3x - 4}{x^2 + 2x - 24} =$

6) $\dfrac{81x^3}{18x} =$

7) $\dfrac{x-3}{x^2 - x - 6} =$

8) $\dfrac{x^2 - 3x - 28}{x-7} =$

9) $\dfrac{6x+18}{30} =$

10) $\dfrac{16}{4x-4} =$

✎ **Identify the points of discontinuity, holes, vertical asymptotes, x–intercepts, and horizontal asymptote of each.**

11) $f(x) = \dfrac{x^3 - x^2 - 6x}{-3x^3 - 3x + 18} =$

12) $f(x) = \dfrac{x^2 + x - 6}{-4x^2 - 16x - 12} =$

13) $f(x) = \dfrac{x-2}{x-4} =$

14) $f(x) = \dfrac{1}{3x^2 + 3x - 18} =$

✎ **Graph rational expressions.**

15) $f(x) = \dfrac{x^2 + 2x - 4}{x-2}$

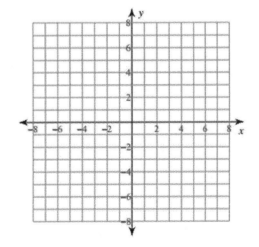

16) $f(x) = \dfrac{4x^3 - 16x + 64}{x^2 - 2x - 4}$

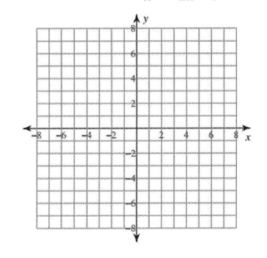

Adding and Subtracting Rational Expressions

✎ *Simplify each expression.*

1) $\dfrac{2}{6x+10} + \dfrac{x-6}{6x+10} =$

9) $\dfrac{2}{x^2-5x+4} + \dfrac{-2}{x^2-4} =$

2) $\dfrac{x+2}{x-4} + \dfrac{x-2}{x+3} =$

10) $\dfrac{4}{x+1} - \dfrac{2}{x+2} =$

3) $\dfrac{3}{x+7} - \dfrac{4}{x-8} =$

11) $\dfrac{5x+5}{5x^2+35x-40} + \dfrac{7x}{3x} =$

4) $\dfrac{x-7}{x^2-16} - \dfrac{x-1}{16-x^2} =$

12) $3 + \dfrac{x}{x+2} - \dfrac{2}{x^2-4} =$

5) $\dfrac{5}{x+5} + \dfrac{4x}{2x+6} =$

13) $\dfrac{4}{x+1} - \dfrac{2}{x+2} =$

6) $2 + \dfrac{x-3}{x+1} =$

14) $\dfrac{2}{3x^2+12x} + \dfrac{8}{2x} =$

7) $\dfrac{2x}{5x+4} + \dfrac{6x}{2x+3} =$

15) $\dfrac{2x}{5x+4} + \dfrac{6x}{2x+3} =$

8) $\dfrac{5xy}{x^2-y^2} - \dfrac{x-y}{x+y} =$

16) $\dfrac{x+5}{4x^2+20x} - \dfrac{x-5}{4x^2+20x} =$

Multiplying and Dividing Rational Expressions

 Simplify each expression.

1) $\dfrac{12x}{14} \times \dfrac{14}{16x} =$

2) $\dfrac{79x}{25} \times \dfrac{85}{27x^2} =$

3) $\dfrac{96}{38x} \times \dfrac{25}{45} =$

4) $\dfrac{84}{3} \times \dfrac{48x}{95} =$

5) $\dfrac{53}{43} \times \dfrac{46}{31}^2 =$

6) $\dfrac{93}{21x} \times \dfrac{34x}{51x} =$

7) $\dfrac{5x + 50}{x + 10} \times \dfrac{x - 2}{5} =$

8) $\dfrac{x - 7}{x + 6} \times \dfrac{10x + 60}{x - 7} =$

9) $\dfrac{1}{x + 10} \times \dfrac{10x + 30}{x + 3} =$

10) $\dfrac{8\,(x+1)}{7x} \times \dfrac{9}{8\,(x+1)} =$

11) $\dfrac{2\,(x + 6)}{4} \times \dfrac{x - 3}{2\,(x - 1)} =$

12) $\dfrac{9\,(x + 4)}{x + 4} \times \dfrac{9x}{9\,(x - 5)} =$

13) $\dfrac{3x^2 + 18}{x + 6} \times \dfrac{1}{x + 8} =$

14) $\dfrac{21x^2 - 21x}{18x^2 - 18x} \times \dfrac{6x}{6x^2} =$

15) $\dfrac{1}{x - 9} \times \dfrac{x^2 + 6x - 27}{x + 9} =$

16) $\dfrac{x^2 - 10x + 25}{10x - 100} \times \dfrac{x - 10}{45 - 9x} =$

 Divide.

1) $\dfrac{8 + 2x - x^2}{x^2 - 2x - 8} \div \dfrac{4x}{x + 6} =$

2) $\dfrac{12}{3} \div \dfrac{5}{8} =$

3) $\dfrac{9a}{a + 5} \div \dfrac{9a}{2a + 10} =$

4) $\dfrac{10x^2}{7} \div \dfrac{3n}{12} =$

5) $\dfrac{11x}{x - 7} \div \dfrac{11x}{12x - 84} =$

6) $\dfrac{x + 10}{9x^2 - 90x} \div \dfrac{1}{9x} =$

7) $\dfrac{x - 2}{x + 6x - 16} \div \dfrac{11x}{x + 9} =$

8) $\dfrac{3x}{x - 5} \div \dfrac{3x}{10x - 50} =$

9) $\dfrac{x + 5}{x + 13x + 40} \div \dfrac{4x}{x + 9} =$

10) $\dfrac{x + 4}{x + 14x + 40} \div \dfrac{6x}{x + 9} =$

11) $\dfrac{14x + 12}{3} \div \dfrac{63x + 54}{3x} =$

12) $\dfrac{7x^3 + 49x^2}{x^2 + 12 + 35} \div \dfrac{2}{2x^3 - 12x^2} =$

13) $\dfrac{x^2 + 10x + 16}{x^2 + 6x + 8} \div \dfrac{1}{x + 8} =$

14) $\dfrac{x^2 - 2x - 15}{8x + 20} \div \dfrac{2}{4x + 10} =$

15) $\dfrac{x - 4}{x^2 - 2x - 8} \div \dfrac{1}{x - 5} =$

16) $\dfrac{1}{2x} \div \dfrac{8x}{2x^2 + 16x} =$

Solving Rational Equations and Complex Fractions

 Solve each equation. Remember to check for extraneous solutions.

1) $\dfrac{2x-3}{x+1} = \dfrac{x+6}{x-2}$

2) $\dfrac{1}{x} = \dfrac{6}{5x} + 1$

3) $\dfrac{2x-3}{x+1} = \dfrac{x+6}{x-2}$

4) $\dfrac{1}{6b^2} + \dfrac{1}{6b} = \dfrac{1}{b^2}$

5) $\dfrac{3x-2}{9x+1} = \dfrac{2x-5}{6x-5}$

6) $\dfrac{1}{n^2} + \dfrac{1}{n} = \dfrac{1}{2n^2}$

7) $\dfrac{1}{8b^2} = \dfrac{1}{4b^2} - \dfrac{1}{b}$

8) $\dfrac{1}{n-8} - 1 = \dfrac{7}{n-8}$

9) $\dfrac{5}{r-2} = -\dfrac{10}{r+2} + 7$

10) $1 = \dfrac{1}{x^2+2x} + \dfrac{x-1}{x}$

11) $\dfrac{1}{x} = 8 + \dfrac{6}{9x}$

12) $\dfrac{x+5}{x^2-2x} - 1 = \dfrac{1}{x^2-2x}$

13) $\dfrac{x-2}{x+3} - 1 = \dfrac{1}{x+2}$

14) $\dfrac{1}{6x^2} = \dfrac{1}{3x^2} - \dfrac{1}{x}$

15) $\dfrac{x+5}{x^2-x} = \dfrac{1}{x^2+x} - \dfrac{x-6}{x+1}$

16) $1 = \dfrac{1}{x^2-2x} + \dfrac{x-1}{x}$

 Simplify each expression.

17) $\dfrac{-1\frac{11}{12}}{-3} =$

18) $\dfrac{\frac{4}{5}}{\frac{2}{25} - \frac{5}{16}} =$

19) $\dfrac{\frac{14}{3}}{-6\frac{2}{11}} =$

20) $\dfrac{9}{\frac{9}{x} + \frac{2}{3x}} =$

21) $\dfrac{x^2}{\frac{4}{5} - \frac{4}{x}} =$

22) $\dfrac{\frac{4}{x-3} - \frac{2}{x+2}}{\frac{8}{x^2+6x+8}} =$

23) $\dfrac{\frac{16}{x-1}}{\frac{16}{5} - \frac{16}{25}} =$

24) $\dfrac{2 + \frac{6}{x-4}}{2 - \frac{4}{x-4}} =$

25) $\dfrac{\frac{1}{2} - \frac{x+5}{4}}{\frac{x^2}{2} - \frac{5}{2}} =$

26) $\dfrac{\frac{x-6}{2} - \frac{x-2}{x-6}}{\frac{36}{x-2} + \frac{4}{9}} =$

Answers of Worksheets – Chapter 11

Simplifying and Graphing rational expressions

1) $\frac{1}{3}$

2) $2(x-3)(x+2)$

3) $\frac{4}{x-1}$

4) $\frac{6}{7}$

5) $\frac{x+1}{x+6}$

6) $\frac{9x^2}{2}$

7) $\frac{x+3}{5}$

8) $x+4$

9) $\frac{x+3}{8}$

10) $\frac{4}{x-1}$

11) Discontinuities: $-3, 2$

Vertical Asym: $x = -3, x = 2$

Holes: None

Horz. Asym: None

X–intercepts: $0, -2, 3$

12) Discontinuities: $-1, -3$

Vertical Asymâ $x = -1$

Holesâ $x = -3$

Horz. Asym: $y = -\frac{1}{4}$

X–intercepts: 2

13) Discontinuities: 4

Vertical Asym: $x = 4$

Holes: None

Horz. Asym: $y = 1$

X–intercepts: 2

14) Discontinuities: $-3, 2$

Vertical Asym: $x = -3, x = 2$

Holes: None

Horz. Asym: $y = 0$

X–intercepts: None

15)

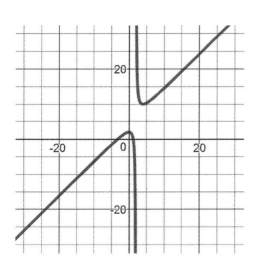

16)

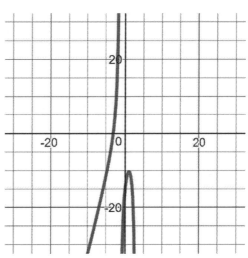

Adding and subtracting rational expressions

1) $\dfrac{-4+x}{6x+10}$

2) $\dfrac{2x^2 - x + 14}{(x-4)(x+3)}$

3) $\dfrac{7x + 4}{(x + 7)(x - 8)}$

4) $\dfrac{2}{x + 4}$

5) $\dfrac{x - 5}{x + 2}$

6) $\dfrac{3x - 1}{x + 1}$

7) $\dfrac{34x^2 + 30}{(5x + 4)(2x + 3)}$

8) $\dfrac{-x^2 + 7xy - y^2}{(x - y)(x + y)}$

9) $\dfrac{10x - 16}{(x^2 - 5x + 4)(x^2 - 4)}$

10) $\dfrac{2x + 6}{(x + 1)(x + 2)}$

11) $\dfrac{52x - 53 + 7x^2}{3(x + 8)(x - 1)}$

12) $\dfrac{4x^2 - 2x - 14}{(x+2)(x-2)}$

13) $\dfrac{2x + 6}{(x + 1)(x + 2)}$

14) $\dfrac{50 + 12x}{3x(x + 4)}$

15) $\dfrac{34x^2 + 30}{(5x + 4)(2x + 3)}$

16) $\dfrac{5}{2x^2 + 10x}$

Multiplying and Dividing rational expressions

1) $\dfrac{4720}{3267}$

2) $\dfrac{1343}{135x}$

3) $\dfrac{80}{57}$

4) $\dfrac{1344x}{95}$

5) $\dfrac{2438x^2}{1333}$

6) $\dfrac{62}{21}$

7) $X - 2$

8) 10

9) $\dfrac{10}{x + 10}$

10) $\dfrac{9}{7x}$

11) $\dfrac{x + 6}{4}$

12) $\dfrac{9x}{x - 5}$

13) $\dfrac{3x}{x + 8}$

14) $\dfrac{7}{6x}$

15) $\dfrac{x - 3}{x - 9}$

16) $-\dfrac{(x - 5)}{90}$

17) $\dfrac{32x}{5}$

18) $6x^2$

19) 2

20) $\frac{40}{7}$

21) 12

22) $\frac{x+10}{x-10}$

23) $\frac{x+9}{11x\,(x+8)}$

24) 10

25) $\frac{2x}{9}$

26) $\frac{x+9}{6x\,(x+10)}$

27) $\frac{2x}{9}$

28) $\frac{14x^4}{x+5}$

29) $x+8$

30) $\frac{(x+3)(x-5)}{4}$

31) $\frac{x-5}{x+2}$

32) $\frac{x+8}{8x}$

Solving rational equations and complex fractions

1) $\left\{\frac{1}{2}\right\}$

2) $\left\{-\frac{1}{5}\right\}$

3) $\{0, 14\}$

4) $\left\{-\frac{15}{16}\right\}$

5) $\left\{\frac{1}{6}\right\}$

6) $\left\{-\frac{1}{2}\right\}$

7) $\left\{\frac{1}{8}\right\}$

8) $\{2\}$

9) $\left\{-\frac{6}{7}, 3\right\}$

10) $\{-1\}$

11) $\left\{\frac{1}{24}\right\}$

12) $\{4, -1\}$

13) $\left\{-\frac{19}{8}\right\}$

14) $\left\{\frac{1}{6}\right\}$

15) $\left\{-\frac{1}{4}\right\}$

16) $\{4, 1\}$

17) $\frac{23}{36}$

18) $-\frac{320}{93}$

19) $-\frac{77}{102}$

20) $\frac{27}{29}$

21) $\frac{5x^2}{4x-20}$

22) $\frac{(x+7)(x+4)}{4\,(x-3)}$

23) $\frac{25}{4x-4}$

24) $\frac{x-1}{x-6}$

25) $\frac{-3-x}{2x^2-10}$

26) $\frac{3x^3-60x^2+252x-288-x}{584x+8x^2-3792}$

Chapter 12: Conic Sections

Topics that you'll learn in this chapter:

✓ Finding the Equation of a Parabola

✓ Finding the Focus, Vertex, and Directrix of a Parabola

✓ Standard Form of a Circle and Finding the Center and the Radius of Circles

✓ Standard Equation of an Ellipse and Finding the Foci, Vertices, and Co–Vertices of Ellipses

✓ Equation of a Hyperbola in Standard Form and Vertices, Co–Vertices, Foci, and Asymptotes of a Hyperbola

✓ Classifying a Conic Section

Finding the Equation of a Parabola

 Write the equation of the following parabolas.

1) Vertex (0, 0) and Focus (0, 2)

2) Vertex (3, 2) and Focus (3, 4)

3) Vertex (1, 1) and Focus (1, 6)

4) Vertex (− 1, 2) and Focus (− 1, 5)

5) Vertex (2, 2) and Focus (2, 6)

6) Vertex (0, 1) and Focus (0, 2)

7) Vertex (2, 1) and Focus (4, 1)

8) Vertex (5, 0) and Focus (9, 0)

9) Vertex (− 2, 4) and Focus (2, 4)

10) Vertex (− 4, 2) and Focus (0, 2)

Finding the Focus, Vertex, and Directrix of a Parabola

✎ *Use the information provided to write the vertex form equation of each parabola.*

1) $y = x^2 + 8x$

2) $y = x^2 - 6x + 5$

3) $y + 6 = (x + 3)^2$

4) $y = x^2 + 10x + 33$

5) $y = (x + 5)(x + 4)$

6) $\frac{1}{2}(y + 4) = (x - 7)^2$

7) $162 + 731 = -y - 9x^2$

8) $y = x^2 + 16x + 71$

9) Focus: $(-\frac{63}{8}, -7)$, Directrix: $x = -\frac{65}{8}$

10) Focus: $(\frac{107}{12}, -7)$, Directrix: $x = \frac{109}{12}$

11) Opens up or down, and passes through $(-6, -7), (-11, -2)$, and $(-8, 1)$

12) Opens up or down, and passes through $(11, 15), (7, 7)$, and $(4, 22)$

Circles

✍ **Write the standard form equation of each circle.**

1) $x^2 + y^2 - 8x - 6y + 21 = 0$
2) $y^2 + 2x + x^2 = 24y - 120$
3) $x^2 + y^2 - 2y - 15 = 0$
4) $8x + x^2 - 2y = 64 - y^2$
5) Center: (–5, –6), Radius: 9
6) Center: (–9, –12), Radius: 4

7) Center: (–12, –5), Area: 4π
8) Center: (–11, –14), Area:16π
9) Center: (–3, 2), Circumference: 2π
10) Center: (15, 14), Circumference: $2π\sqrt{15}$

✍ **Identify the center and radius of each. Then sketch the graph.**

11) $(x - 2)^2 + (y + 5)^2 = 10$

12) $x^2 + (y - 1)^2 = 4$

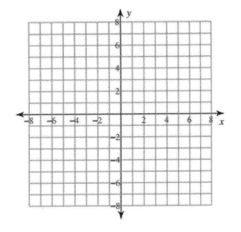
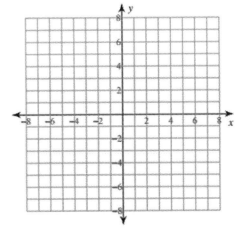

13) $(x - 2)^2 + (y + 6)^2 = 9$

14) $(x + 14)^2 + (y - 5)^2 = 16$

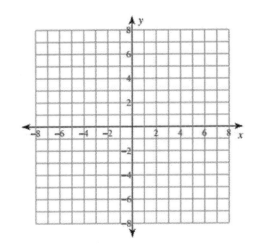

Ellipses

🖎 **Use the information provided to write the standard form equation of each ellipse.**

1) Foci: $(2\sqrt{3}, 0)$, $(-2\sqrt{3}, 0)$
   Co–vertices: $(0, 2)$. $(0, -2)$

2) Vertices: $(0, 6)$, $(0, -6)$
   Co–vertices: $(3, 0)$. $(-3, 0)$

3) Vertices: $(4, 3)$, $(4, -7)$
   Co–vertices: $(1, -2)$. $(7, -2)$

4) Foci: $(\sqrt{17}, 0)$, $(-\sqrt{17}, 0)$
   Co–vertices: $(9, 0)$. $(-9, 0)$

5) Foci: $(-7, 5 + \sqrt{13})$, $(-7, 5 - \sqrt{13})$
   Co–vertices: $(-1, 5)$. $(-13, 5)$

6) Vertices: $(5, 1)$, $(-1, 1)$
   Co–vertices: $(2, 3)$. $(2, -1)$

7) Vertices: $(12, 0)$, $(-12, 0)$
   Co–vertices: $(2\sqrt{11}, 0)$. $(-2\sqrt{11}, 0)$

8) Vertices: $(7 + 2\sqrt{35}, -4)$, $(7 - 2\sqrt{35}, -4)$
   Co–vertices: $(7, -2)$. $(7, -6)$

9) Center: $(4, 8)$
   Vertex: $(4, 8 -\sqrt{170})$
   Co–vertex: $(4 - \sqrt{15}, 8)$

10) Center: $(7, -10)$
    Vertex: $(-6, -10)$
    Co–vertex: $(7, -17)$

🖎 **Identify the vertices, co–vertices, foci.**

11) $\dfrac{x^2}{169} + \dfrac{y^2}{64} = 1$

12) $\dfrac{x^2}{95} + \dfrac{y^2}{30} = 1$

13) $\dfrac{x^2}{36} + \dfrac{y^2}{16} = 1$

14) $\dfrac{x^2}{49} + \dfrac{y^2}{169} = 1$

15) $\dfrac{(x+5)^2}{81} + \dfrac{(y-1)^2}{144} = 1$

16) $\dfrac{(x-3)^2}{49} + \dfrac{(y-9)^2}{4} = 1$

17) $\dfrac{x^2}{64} + \dfrac{(y-8)^2}{9} = 1$

18) $\dfrac{x^2}{64} + \dfrac{(y-6)^2}{121} = 1$

Hyperbola

✎ ***Use the information provided to write the standard form equation of each hyperbola.***

1) $-2x^2 + 3y^2 + 4x - 60y + 268 = 0$

2) $-x^2 + y^2 - 18x - 14y - 132 = 0$

3) $-16x^2 + 9y^2 + 32x + 144y - 16 = 0$

4) $9x^2 - 4y^2 - 90x + 32y - 163 = 0$

5) Vertices: $(8, 14)$, $(8, -10)$, Conjugate Axis is 6 units long

6) Vertices: $(7, 4)$, $(7, -24)$, Distance from Center to Focus $= 7\sqrt{5}$

7) Vertices: $(-5, 22)$, $(-5, -4)$, Distance from Center to Focus $= \sqrt{218}$

8) Vertices: $(0, -1)$, $(-20, -1)$, Asymptotes: $y = x + 9$, $y = -x - 11$

9) Foci: $(-9, -5 + 9\sqrt{2})$, $(-9, -5 - 9\sqrt{2})$, Conjugate Axis is 18 units long

10) Foci: $(8, -5 + \sqrt{53})$, $(8, -5 - \sqrt{53})$,

    Endpoints of Conjugate Axis: $(15, -5)$, $(1, -5)$

✎ ***Identify the vertices, foci, and direction of opening of each.***

11) $\dfrac{y^2}{25} - \dfrac{x^2}{16} = 1$

12) $\dfrac{x^2}{121} - \dfrac{y^2}{36} = 1$

13) $\dfrac{x^2}{121} - \dfrac{y^2}{81} = 1$

14) $\dfrac{x^2}{81} - \dfrac{y^2}{4} = 1$

15) $\dfrac{(x+2)^2}{169} - \dfrac{(y+8)^2}{4} = 1$

16) $\dfrac{(y+8)^2}{36} - \dfrac{(y+2)^2}{25} = 1$

Writing the Equation of a Hyperbola in Standard Form

✍ *Use the information provided to write the standard form equation of each hyperbola.*

1) $-2x^2 + 3y^2 + 4x - 60y + 268 = 0$

2) $-x^2 + y^2 - 18x - 14y - 132 = 0$

3) $-16x^2 + 9y^2 + 32x + 144y - 16 = 0$

4) $9x^2 - 4y^2 - 90x + 32y - 163 = 0$

5) Vertices: (8, 14), (8, −10), Conjugate Axis is 6 units long

6) Vertices: (7, 4), (7, −24), Distance from Center to Focus = $7\sqrt{5}$

7) Vertices: (−5, 22), (−5, −4), Distance from Center to Focus = $\sqrt{218}$

8) Vertices: (0, −1), (−20, −1), Asymptotes: $y = x + 9$, $y = -x - 11$

9) Foci: (−9, −5 + $9\sqrt{2}$), (−9, −5 − $9\sqrt{2}$), Conjugate Axis is 18 units long

10) Foci: (8, −5 + $\sqrt{53}$), (8, −5 − $\sqrt{53}$),

   Endpoints of Conjugate Axis: (15, −5), (1, −5)

Classifying a Conic Section (in Standard Form)

✍ *Classify each conic section and write its equation in standard form.*

1) $x^2 - 4y^2 + 6x - 8y + 1 = 0$

2) $3x^2 + 3x + y + 79 = 0$

3) $x^2 + y^2 + 4x - 2y - 18 = 0$

4) $-y^2 + x + 8y - 17 = 0$

5) $49x^2 + 9y^2 + 392x + 343 = 0$

6) $-9x^2 + y^2 - 72x - 153 = 0$

7) $-2y^2 + x - 20y - 49 = 0$

8) $-x^2 + 10x + y - 21 = 0$

✍ *Classify each conic section. (Not in Standard Form)*

1) $x^2 + y^2 - 8x + 8y - 4 = 0$

2) $y = 6x^2 - 60x + 149$

3) $x^2 - 4x + 4y^2 - 32y + 32 = 0$

4) $x^2 - 2x - 36y^2 - 360y - 935 = 0$

5) $y = 6x^2 - 60x + 149$

6) $x^2 + y^2 - 8x + 8y - 4 = 0$

7) $x^2 + y^2 + 6x + 10y + 33 = 0$

8) $x^2 - 4x - 36y^2 + 288y - 608 = 0$

9) $9x^2 + 4y^2 + 16y - 128 = 0$

10) $x^2 + 8x - 25y^2 + 50y - 34 = 0$

11) $y = 6x^2 + 60x + 155$

12) $4x^2 + 9y^2 - 54y + 45 = 0$

13) $-9x^2 - 54x + 4y^2 - 40y - 125 = 0$

14) $x^2 - 4x + 4y^2 - 32y + 32 = 0$

Answers of Worksheets – Chapter 12

Finding the Equation of a Parabola

Write the equation of the following parabolas.

1) Vertex (0, 0) and Focus (0, 2): $x^2 = 8y$

2) Vertex (3, 2) and Focus (3, 4): $(x - 3)^2 = 8 (y- 2)$

3) Vertex (1, 1) and Focus (1, 6): $(x - 1)^2 = 20 (y - 1)$

4) Vertex (– 1, 2) and Focus (– 1, 5): $(x + 1)^2 = 12 (y - 2)$

5) Vertex (2, 2) and Focus (2, 6): $(x - 2)^2 = 8 (y - 2)$

6) Vertex (0, 1) and Focus (0, 2): $x^2 = 8 (y - 1)$

7) Vertex (2, 1) and Focus (4, 1): $(y - 1)^2 = 8 (x - 2)$

8) Vertex (5, 0) and Focus (9, 0): $(y - 1)^2 = 8 (x - 2)$

9) Vertex (– 2, 4) and Focus (2, 4): $(y - 4)^2 = 16 (x + 2)$

10) Vertex (– 4, 2) and Focus (0, 2): $(y + 4)^2 = 16x$

Finding the Focus, Vertex, and the Directrix of a Parabola

11) $y = (x + 4)^2 - 16$

12) $y = (x - 3)^2 - 4$

13) $y = (x + 3)^2 - 6$

14) $y = (x + 5)^2 + 8$

15) $y = (x + \frac{9}{2})^2 - \frac{1}{4}$

16) $y = 2 (x - 7)^2 - 4$

17) $y = -9 (x + 9)^2 - 2$

18) $y = (x + 8)^2 + 7$

19) $x = 2 (y + 7)^2 - 8$

20) $x = -3 (y + 7)^2 + 9$

21) $y = - (x + 9)^2 + 2$

22) $y = (x - 8)^2 + 6$

Circles

1) $(x - 4)^2 + (y - 3)^2 = 4$

2) $(x + 1)^2 + (y - 12)^2 = 25$

3) $x^2 + (y - 1)^2 = 16$

4) $(x + 4)^2 + (y - 1)^2 = 81$

5) $(x + 5)^2 + (y + 6)^2 = 81$

6) $(x + 9)^2 + (y + 12)^2 = 16$

7) $(x + 12)^2 + (y + 5)^2 = 4$

8) $(x + 11)^2 + (y + 14)^2 = 16$

9) $(x + 3)^2 + (y - 2)^2 = 1$

10) $(x - 15)^2 + (y - 14)^2 = 15$

11) Center: (2, −5), Radius: $\sqrt{10}$

12) Center: (0, 1), Radius: $2\sqrt{26}$

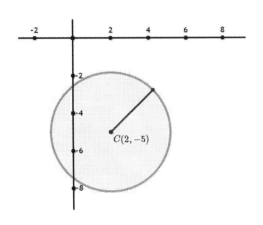

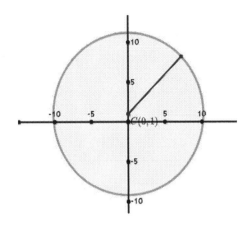

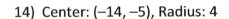

13) Center: (2, − 6), Radius: 3

14) Center: (−14, −5), Radius: 4

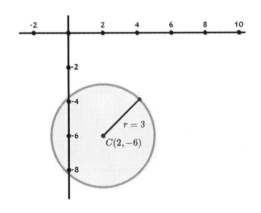

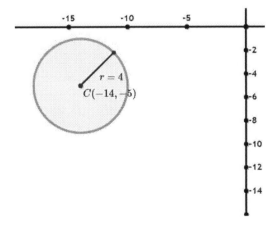

Ellipses

1) $\dfrac{x^2}{16} + \dfrac{y^2}{4} = 1$

2) $\dfrac{x^2}{9} + \dfrac{y^2}{36} = 1$

3) $\dfrac{(x-4)^2}{9} + \dfrac{(y+2)^2}{25} = 1$

4) $\dfrac{x^2}{81} + \dfrac{y^2}{64} = 1$

5) $\dfrac{(x+7)^2}{36} + \dfrac{(y-5)^2}{49} = 1$

6) $\dfrac{(x-2)^2}{9} + \dfrac{(y-1)^2}{4} = 1$

7) $\dfrac{x^2}{144} + \dfrac{y^2}{100} = 1$

8) $\dfrac{(x-7)^2}{144} + \dfrac{(y+5)^2}{4} = 1$

9) $\dfrac{(x-4)^2}{15} + \dfrac{(y-8)^2}{170} = 1$

10) $\dfrac{(x-7)^2}{169} + \dfrac{(y+10)^2}{49} = 1$

11) Vertices: (13, 0), (−13, 0)

Co−vertices: (0, 8), (0, −8)

Foci: ($\sqrt{105}$, 0), (−$\sqrt{105}$, 0)

12) Vertices: ($\sqrt{95}$, 0), (−$\sqrt{95}$, 0)

Co−vertices: (0, $\sqrt{30}$), (0, −$\sqrt{30}$)

Foci: ($\sqrt{65}$, 0), (−$\sqrt{65}$, 0)

13) Vertices: (6, 0), (−6, 0)

Co−vertices: (0,4), (0, −4)

Foci: ($2\sqrt{5}$, 0), (−$2\sqrt{5}$, 0)

14) Vertices: (0, 13), (0, −13)

Co−vertices: (7, 0), (−7, 0)

Foci: (0, $2\sqrt{30}$), (0, −$2\sqrt{30}$)

15) Vertices: (−5, 13), (−5, −11)

Co−vertices: (4, 1), (−14, 1)

Foci: (−5, $1 + 3\sqrt{7}$), (−5, $1 - 3\sqrt{7}$)

16) Vertices: (10, 9), (−4, 9)

Co−vertices: (3, 11), (3, 7)

Foci: ($3 + 3\sqrt{5}$, 9), ($3 - 3\sqrt{5}$, 9)

17) Vertices: (8, 8), (−8, 8)

Co−vertices: (0, 11), (0, 5)

Foci: ($\sqrt{55}$, 8), (−$\sqrt{55}$, 8)

18) Vertices: (0, 17), (0, −5)

Co−vertices: (8, 6), (−8, 6)

Foci: (0, $6 + \sqrt{57}$), (0, $6 - \sqrt{57}$)

Hyperbola

1) $\dfrac{(y-1)^2}{10} - \dfrac{(x-1)^2}{15} = 1$

2) $\dfrac{(y-7)^2}{100} - \dfrac{(x+9)^2}{100} = 1$

3) $\dfrac{(y+8)^2}{64} - \dfrac{(x-1)^2}{36} = 1$

4) $\dfrac{(x-5)^2}{36} - \dfrac{(y-4)^2}{81} = 1$

5) $\dfrac{(y-2)^2}{144} - \dfrac{(x-8)^2}{9} = 1$

6) $\dfrac{(y+10)^2}{196} - \dfrac{(x-7)^2}{49} = 1$

7) $\dfrac{(y-9)^2}{196} - \dfrac{(x+5)^2}{49} = 1$

8) $\dfrac{(x+10)^2}{100} - \dfrac{(y+1)^2}{100} = 1$

9) $\dfrac{(y+5)^2}{81} - \dfrac{(x+9)^2}{81} = 1$

10) $\dfrac{(y+5)^2}{4} - \dfrac{(x-8)^2}{49} = 1$

11) Vertices: $(0, 5)$, $(0, -5)$

Foci: $(0, \sqrt{41})$, $(0, -\sqrt{41})$

Opens up/down

12) Vertices: $(11, 0)$, $(-11, 0)$

Foci: $(\sqrt{157}, 0)$, $(-\sqrt{157}, 0)$

Opens left/right

13) Vertices: $(11, 0)$, $(-11, 0)$

Foci: $(\sqrt{202}, 0)$, $(-\sqrt{202}, 0)$

Opens left/right

14) Vertices: $(9, 0)$, $(-9, 0)$

Foci: $(\sqrt{85}, 0)$, $(-\sqrt{85}, 0)$

Opens left/right

15) Vertices: $(11, -8)$, $(-15, -8)$

Foci: $(-2 + \sqrt{173}, -8)$, $(-2 - \sqrt{173}, -8)$

Opens left/right

16) Vertices: $(-2, -2)$, $(-2, -14)$

Foci: $(-2, -8 + \sqrt{61})$, $(-2, -8 - \sqrt{61})$

Opens up/down

Classifying a Conic Section

1) Hyperbola, $\dfrac{(x+3)^2}{4} - (y+1)^2 = 1$
2) Parabola, $y = -3(x+5)^2 - 4$
3) Circle, $(x+2)^2 + (y-1)^2 = 23$
4) Parabola, $x = (y-4)^2 + 1$
5) Ellipse, $\dfrac{(x+4)^2}{9} + \dfrac{y^2}{49} = 1$
6) Hyperbola, $\dfrac{y^2}{9} - (x+4)^2 = 1$
7) Parabola, $x = 2(y+5)^2 - 1$
8) Parabola, $y = (x-5)^2 - 4$
9) Circle

10) Parabola

11) Ellipse

12) Hyperbola

13) Parabola

14) Circle

15) Circle

16) Hyperbola

17) Ellipse

18) Hyperbola

19) Parabola

20) Ellipse

21) Hyperbola

22) Ellipse

Chapter 13: Trigonometric Functions

Topics that you'll practice in this chapter:

- ✓ Trig ratios of General Angles
- ✓ Sketch Each Angle in Standard Position
- ✓ Finding Co–Terminal Angles and Reference Angles
- ✓ Angles in Radians
- ✓ Angles in Degrees
- ✓ Evaluating Each Trigonometric Expression
- ✓ Missing Sides and Angles of a Right Triangle
- ✓ Arc Length and Sector Area

Mathematics is like checkers in being suitable for the young, not too difficult, amusing, and

without peril to the state. — Plato

Trig ratios of General Angles

✍ *Evaluate.*

1) $\sin -60° =$ _____

2) $\sin 150° =$ _____

3) $\cos 315° =$ _____

4) $\cos 180° =$ _____

5) $\sin 120° =$ _____

6) $\sin -330° =$ _____

7) $\tan -90° =$ _____

8) $\cot 90° =$ _____

9) $\tan 270° =$ _____

10) $\cot 150° =$ _____

11) $\sec 120° =$ _____

12) $\csc -360° =$ _____

13) $\cot -270° =$ _____

14) $\sec 90° =$ _____

15) $\cos -90° =$ _____

16) $\sec 60° =$ _____

17) $\csc 480° =$ _____

18) $\cot -135° =$ _____

✍ **Find the exact value of each trigonometric function. Some may be undefined.**

19) $\sec \pi =$ _____

20) $\tan -\dfrac{3\pi}{2} =$ _____

21) $\cos \dfrac{11\pi}{6} =$ _____

22) $\cot \dfrac{5\pi}{3} =$ _____

23) $\sec -\dfrac{3\pi}{4} =$ _____

24) $\sec \dfrac{\pi}{3} =$ _____

25) $\csc \dfrac{5\pi}{6} =$ _____

26) $\cot \dfrac{4\pi}{3} =$ _____

27) $\csc -\dfrac{3\pi}{4} =$ _____

28) $\cot \dfrac{2\pi}{3} =$ _____

Sketch Each Angle in Standard Position

 Draw each angle with the given measure in standard position.

1) −120°

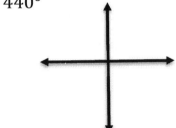

4) 280°

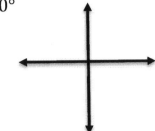

2) 440°

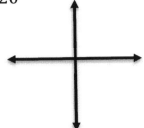

5) 710°

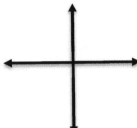

3) $-\dfrac{10\pi}{3}$

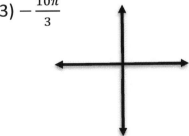

6) $\dfrac{11\pi}{6}$

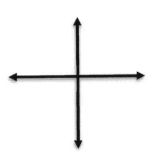

Finding Co-terminal Angles and Reference Angles

 Find a conterminal angle between 0° and 360° for each angle provided.

1) $-440° =$

2) $640° =$

3) $-435° =$

4) $-330° =$

 Find a conterminal angle between 0 and 2π for each given angle.

5) $\dfrac{15\pi}{4} =$

6) $-\dfrac{19\pi}{12} =$

7) $-\dfrac{35\pi}{18} =$

8) $\dfrac{11}{3} =$

 Find the reference angle of each angle.

9)

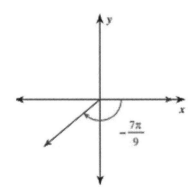

$-\dfrac{7\pi}{9}$

$640°$

10)

Angles and Angle Measure

✎ **Convert each degree measure into radians.**

1) $-140° =$ ___

2) $320° =$ ___

3) $210° =$ ___

4) $780° =$ ___

5) $-190° =$ ___

6) $345° =$ ___

7) $-150° =$ ___

8) $420° =$ ___

9) $300° =$ ___

10) $-60° =$ ___

11) $315° =$ ___

12) $600° =$ ___

13) $-720° =$ ___

14) $-160° =$ ___

15) $-210° =$ ___

16) $960° =$ ___

17) $-30° =$ ___

18) $660° =$ ___

19) $-240° =$ ___

20) $840° =$ ___

21) $1,200° =$ ___

✎ **Convert each radian measure into degrees.**

22) $\dfrac{\pi}{30} =$

23) $\dfrac{4\pi}{5} =$

24) $\dfrac{7\pi}{18} =$

25) $\dfrac{\pi}{5} =$

26) $-\dfrac{5\pi}{4} =$

27) $\dfrac{14\pi}{3} =$

28) $-\dfrac{16\pi}{3} =$

29) $-\dfrac{3\pi}{5} =$

30) $\dfrac{11\pi}{6} =$

31) $\dfrac{5\pi}{9} =$

32) $-\dfrac{\pi}{3} =$

33) $\dfrac{13\pi}{6} =$

34) $\dfrac{9\pi}{4} =$

35) $\dfrac{21\pi}{4} =$

36) $-\dfrac{4\pi}{15} =$

37) $\dfrac{14}{3} =$

38) $-\dfrac{41\pi}{12} =$

39) $-\dfrac{17}{9} =$

Evaluating Trigonometric Functions

✎ **Find the exact value of each trigonometric function.**

1) $\cos 225° = $ _____

2) $\tan \dfrac{7\pi}{6} = $

3) $\tan -\dfrac{\pi}{6} = $ _____

4) $\cot -\dfrac{7\pi}{6} = $ _____

5) $\cos -\dfrac{\pi}{4} = $ _____

6) $\cos -480° = $ _____

7) $\sin 690° = $ _____

8) $\tan 420° = $ _____

9) $\cot - 495° = $ _____

10) $\tan 405° = $ _____

11) $\cot 390° = $ _____

12) $\cos - 300° = $ _____

13) $\cot - 210° = $ _____

✎ **Use the given point on the terminal side of angle θ to find the value of the trigonometric function indicated.**

14) $\sin\theta; \ (-6, 4)$

15) $\cos\theta; \ (2, -2)$

16) $\cot\theta; \ (-7, \sqrt{15})$

17) $\cos\theta; \ (-5, -12)$

18) $\sin\theta; \ (-\sqrt{7}, 3)$

19) $\tan\theta; \ (-11, -2)$

Missing Sides and Angles of a Right Triangle

✍ *Find the value of each trigonometric ratio as fractions in their simplest form.*

1) $\tan A$

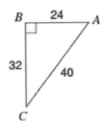

2) $\sin x$

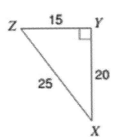

✍ *Find the missing sides. Round answers to the nearest tenth.*

3)

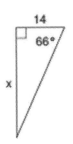

4)

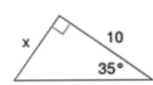

5)

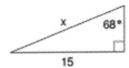

6)

Arc Length and Sector Area

✎ **Find the length of each arc. Round your answers to the nearest tenth.**

($π = 3.14$)

1) $r = 28$ cm, $θ = 45°$

3) $r = 22$ ft, $θ = 60°$

2) $r = 15$ ft, $θ = 95°$

4) $r = 12$ m, $θ = 85°$

✎ **Find area of each sector. Do not round. Round your answers to the nearest tenth.** ($π = 3.14$)

5)

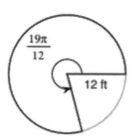

6)

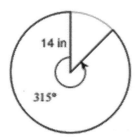

7)

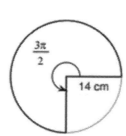

8)

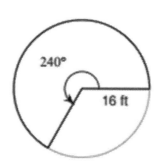

Answers of Worksheets – Chapter 16

Trig Ratios of General Angles

1) $-\frac{\sqrt{3}}{2}$

2) $\frac{1}{2}$

3) $\frac{\sqrt{2}}{2}$

4) -1

5) $\frac{\sqrt{3}}{2}$

6) $\frac{1}{2}$

7) Undefined

8) 0

9) Undefined

10) $-\sqrt{3}$

11) -2

12) 1

13) 0

14) Undefined

15) 0

16) 2

17) $\frac{2\sqrt{3}}{3}$

18) 1

19) -1

20) Undefined

21) $\frac{\sqrt{3}}{2}$

22) $-\frac{\sqrt{3}}{3}$

23) $-\sqrt{2}$

24) 2

25) 2

26) $\frac{\sqrt{3}}{3}$

27) $-\sqrt{2}$

28) $-\frac{\sqrt{3}}{3}$

Sketch Each Angle in Standard Position

1) $-120°$

2) $440°$

3) $-\frac{10\pi}{3}$

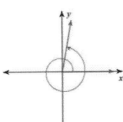

4) $280°$

5) $710°$

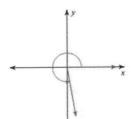
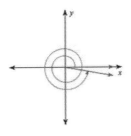
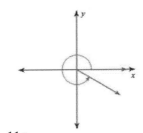

6) $\frac{11\pi}{6}$

Finding Co–Terminal Angles and Reference Angles

1) 280°

2) 280°

3) 285°

4) 30°

5) $\frac{7\pi}{4}$

6) $\frac{5\pi}{12}$

7) $\frac{\pi}{18}$

8) $\frac{5\pi}{3}$

9) $\frac{2\pi}{9}$

10) 80°

Angles and Angle Measure

1) $-\frac{7\pi}{9}$

2) $\frac{16}{9}$

3) $\frac{7\pi}{6}$

4) $\frac{13}{3}$

5) $-\frac{19}{18}$

6) $\frac{23\pi}{12}$

7) $-\frac{5\pi}{6}$

8) $\frac{7\pi}{3}$

9) $\frac{5\pi}{3}$

10) $-\frac{\pi}{3}$

11) $\frac{7\pi}{4}$

12) $\frac{10\pi}{3}$

13) -4π

14) $-\frac{8\pi}{9}$

15) $-\frac{7\pi}{6}$

16) $\frac{16}{3}$

17) $-\frac{\pi}{6}$

18) $\frac{11\pi}{3}$

19) $-\frac{4\pi}{3}$

20) $\frac{14\pi}{3}$

21) $\frac{20}{3}$

22) 6°

23) 144°

24) 70°

25) 36°

26) −225°

27) 840°

28) −960°

29) −108°

30) 330°

31) 100°

32) −60°

33) 390°

34) 405°

35) 945°

36) −48°

37) 840°

38) −615°

39) −340°

Evaluating Each Trigonometric Expression

1) $-\frac{\sqrt{2}}{2}$

2) $\frac{\sqrt{3}}{3}$

3) $-\frac{\sqrt{3}}{3}$

4) $-\sqrt{3}$

5) $\frac{\sqrt{2}}{2}$

6) $-\frac{1}{2}$

7) $-\frac{1}{2}$

8) $\sqrt{3}$

9) 1

10) 1

11) $\sqrt{3}$

12) $\frac{1}{2}$

13) $-\sqrt{3}$

14) $\frac{2\sqrt{13}}{13}$

16) $-\frac{7\sqrt{15}}{15}$

18) $\frac{3}{4}$

15) $\sqrt{2}$

17) $-\frac{5}{13}$

19) $\frac{2}{11}$

Missing Sides and Angles of a Right Triangle

1) $\frac{4}{3}$

4) 7.0

5) 16.2

2) $\frac{3}{5}$

6) 31.1

3) 31.4

Arc Length and Sector Area

1) 22 cm

4) 17.8 m

7) 461.6 cm^2

2) 24.9 ft

5) 358 ft^2

535.9 ft^2

3) 23 ft

6) 538.5 in^2

Chapter 14: Statistics and Probabilities

Topics that you'll learn in this chapter:

- ✓ Probability of Simple Events
- ✓ Factorials
- ✓ Permutations
- ✓ Combination

Probability Problems

✎ *Solve.*

1) A number is chosen at random from 1 to 10. Find the probability of selecting number 4 or smaller numbers. _____

2) Bag A contains 9 red marbles and 3 green marbles. Bag B contains 9 black marbles and 6 orange marbles. What is the probability of selecting a green marble at random from bag A? What is the probability of selecting a black marble at random from Bag B? _____ _____

3) A number is chosen at random from 1 to 50. What is the probability of selecting multiples of 10. _____

4) A card is chosen from a well-shuffled deck of 52 cards. What is the probability that the card will be a king OR a queen? _____

5) A number is chosen at random from 1 to 10. What is the probability of selecting a multiple of 3. _____

A spinner, numbered 1-8, is spun once. What is the probability of spinning …

6) an EVEN number? _____   7) a multiple of 3? _____

8) a PRIME number? _____   9) number 9? _____

Factorials

✎ *Determine the value for each expression.*

1) $3! + 2! =$

2) $3! + 6! =$

3) $(3!)^2 =$

4) $5! + 4! =$

5) $4! - 5! + 4 =$

6) $2! \times 5 - 12 =$

7) $(2! + 1!)^3 =$

8) $(3! + 0!)^3 =$

9) $(2!\, 0!)^4 - 1 =$

10) $\dfrac{7!}{4!} =$

11) $\dfrac{9!}{6!} =$

12) $\dfrac{8!}{5!} =$

13) $\dfrac{7!}{5!} =$

14) $\dfrac{20!}{18!} =$

15) $\dfrac{10!}{8!} =$

16) $\dfrac{(5+1!)^3}{3!} =$

17) $\dfrac{25!}{20!} =$

18) $\dfrac{22!}{18!5!} =$

19) $\dfrac{10!}{8!2!} =$

20) $\dfrac{100!}{97!} =$

21) $\dfrac{14!}{10!4!} =$

22) $\dfrac{14!}{9!3!} =$

23) $\dfrac{55!}{53!} =$

24) $\dfrac{(2 .3)!}{3!} =$

25) $\dfrac{4!(9n-1)!}{(9n)!} =$

26) $\dfrac{n(3n+8)!}{(3n+9)!} =$

27) $\dfrac{(n-2)!(n-1)}{(n+1)!} =$

Combinations and Permutations

✎ **Calculate the value of each.**

1) $4! = $ ____

2) $4! \times 3! = $ ____

3) $5! = $ ____

4) $6! + 3! = $ ____

5) $7! = $ ____

6) $8! = $ ____

7) $4! + 4! = $ ____

8) $4! - 3! = $ ____

✎ **Solve each word problems.**

9) Susan is baking cookies. She uses sugar, flour, butter, and eggs. How many different orders of ingredients can she try? _____

10) Jason is planning for his vacation. He wants to go to museum, watch a movie, go to the beach, and play volleyball. How many different ways of ordering are there for him? _____

11) How many 5-digit numbers can be named using the digits 1, 2, 3, 4, and 5 without repetition? _____

12) In how many ways can 5 boys be arranSAT in a straight line? _____

13) In how many ways can 4 athletes be arranSAT in a straight line? _____

14) A professor is going to arrange her 7 students in a straight line. In how many ways can she do this? _____

15) How many code symbols can be formed with the letters for the word WHITE? _____

16) In how many ways a team of 8 basketball players can to choose a captain and co-captain? _____

Answers of Worksheets – Chapter 14

Probability Problems

1) $\frac{2}{5}$

2) $\frac{1}{4}, \frac{3}{5}$

3) $\frac{1}{5}$

4) $\frac{2}{13}$

5) $\frac{3}{10}$

6) $\frac{1}{2}$

7) $\frac{1}{4}$

8) $\frac{1}{2}$

9) 0

Factorials

1) 8
2) 726
3) 36
4) 144
5) −92
6) −2
7) 27
8) 125
9) 15
10) 210

11) 504
12) 336
13) 42
14) 380
15) 90
16) 36
17) 6,375,600
18) 1,463
19) 45
20) 970,200

21) 1,001
22) 40,040
23) 2,970
24) 120
25) $\frac{8}{3n}$
26) $\frac{n}{3(n+3)}$
27) $\frac{1}{n(n+1)}$

Combinations and Permutations

1) 24
2) 144
3) 120
4) 726
5) 5,040
6) 40,320

7) 48
8) 18
9) 24
10) 24
11) 120
12) 120

13) 24
14) 5,040
15) 120
16) 56

Chapter 15: Sequences and Series

Topics that you'll practice in this chapter:

- ✓ Arithmetic Sequences
- ✓ Geometric Sequences
- ✓ Comparing Arithmetic and Geometric Sequences
- ✓ Finite Geometric Series
- ✓ Infinite Geometric Series

Mathematics is like checkers in being suitable for the young, not too difficult, amusing, and without peril to the state. — Plato

Arithmetic Sequences

✍ **Find the next three terms of each arithmetic sequence.**

1) $15, 11, 7, 3, -1, \ldots$

2) $-21, -14, -7, 0, \ldots$

3) $3, 6, 9, 12, 15, \ldots$

4) $4, 8, 12, 16, 20, \ldots$

✍ **Given the first term and the common difference of an arithmetic sequence find the first five terms and the explicit formula.**

5) $a_1 = 24, d = 2$

6) $a_1 = -15, d = -5$

7) $a_1 = 18, d = 10$

8) $a_1 = -38, d = -100$

✍ **Given a term in an arithmetic sequence and the common difference find the first five terms and the explicit formula.**

9) $a_{36} = -276, d = -7$

10) $a_{37} = 249, d = 8$

11) $a_{38} = -53.2, d = -1.1$

12) $a_{40} = -1,191, d = -30$

✍ **Given a term in an arithmetic sequence and the common difference find the recursive formula and the three terms in the sequence after the last one given.**

13) $a_{22} = -44, d = -2$

14) $a_{12} = 28.6, d = 1.8$

15) $a_{18} = 27.4, d = 1.1$

16) $a_{21} = -1.4, d = 0.6$

Geometric Sequences

✎ **Determine if the sequence is geometric. If it is, find the common ratio.**

1) $1, -5, 25, -125, \dots$

2) $-2, -4, -8, -16, \dots$

3) $4, 16, 36, 64, \dots$

4) $-3, -15, -75, -375, \dots$

✎ **Given the first term and the common ratio of a geometric sequence find the first five terms and the explicit formula.**

5) $a_1 = 0.8, r = -5$

6) $a_1 = 1, r = 2$

✎ **Given the recursive formula for a geometric sequence find the common ratio, the first five terms, and the explicit formula.**

7) $a_n = a_{n-1} \cdot 2, a_1 = 2$

8) $a_n = a_{n-1} \cdot -3, a_1 = -3$

9) $a_n = a_{n-1} \cdot 5, a_1 = 2$

10) $a_n = a_{n-1} \cdot 3, a_1 = -3$

✎ **Given two terms in a geometric sequence find the 8th term and the recursive formula.**

11) $a_4 = 12$ and $a_5 = -6$

12) $a_5 = 768$ and $a_2 = 12$

Comparing Arithmetic and Geometric Sequences

✏️ *For each sequence, state if it is arithmetic, geometric, or neither.*

1) $4, 7, 10, 13, \ldots$

2) $2, 8, 14, 20, \ldots$

3) $1, 7, 15, 31, \ldots$

4) $0, 3, 8, 15, 24, \ldots$

5) $4, 16, 36, 64, 10, \ldots$

6) $1, 4, 9, 16, 25, \ldots$

7) $1, 5, 25, 125, 625, \ldots$

8) $4, 36, 64, 100, \ldots$

9) $-29, -34, -39, -44, -49, \ldots$

10) $-4, 12, -36, 108, -324, \ldots$

11) $40, 43, 46, 49, 52, \ldots$

12) $1, 3, 6, 10, 15, \ldots$

13) $-34, -26, -18, -10, -2, \ldots$

14) $a_n = 5 \cdot 3^{n-1}$

15) $a_n = 3 \cdot 3^{n-1}$

16) $a_n = 5 - 4n$

17) $a_n = -163 + 200_n$

18) $a_n = 16 + 3_n$

19) $a_n = -4 \cdot (-3)^{n-1}$

20) $a_n = -43 + 4_n$

21) $a_n = (2n)^2$

22) $a_n = -43 + 7_n$

23) $a_n = -(-3)^{n-1}$

24) $a_n = 2 \cdot (-3)^{n-1}$

25) $a_n = \dfrac{n}{2^n}$

26) $a_n = \dfrac{5 - 5n}{3^n}$

27) $a_n = \dfrac{7 - 5n}{2^n}$

28) $a_n = \dfrac{6 - a_{n-1}}{4}$

29) $a_n = -\dfrac{3}{4} + \dfrac{3}{2}n$

Finite Geometric Series

 Evaluate the related series of each sequence.

1) $-1, 5, -25, 125$

2) $-2, 6, -18, 54, -162$

3) $-1, 4, -16, 64$

4) $2, 12, 72, 432$

5) $-4, -8, -16, -32, -64$

6) $1, 5, 25, 125, 625$

 Evaluate each geometric series described.

7) $1 + 2 + 4 + 8 \ldots, n = 6$ _____

8) $1 - 4 + 16 - 64 \ldots, n = 9$ _____

9) $-2 - 6 - 18 - 54 \ldots, n = 9$ _____

10) $2 - 10 + 50 - 250 \ldots, n = 8$ _____

11) $1 - 5 + 25 - 125 \ldots, n = 7$ _____

12) $-3 - 6 - 12 - 24 \ldots, n = 9$ _____

13) $a_1 = -1, r = 4, n = 8$ _____

14) $a_1 = -2, r = -3, n = 9$ _____

15) $\sum_{n=1}^{8} 2 \cdot (-2)^{n-1}$ _____

16) $\sum_{n=1}^{9} 4 \cdot 3^{n-1}$ _____

17) $\sum_{n=1}^{10} 4 \cdot (-3)^{n-1}$ _____

18) $\sum_{m=1}^{9} -2^{m-1}$ _____

19) $\sum_{m=1}^{8} 3 \cdot 5^{m-1}$ _____

20) $\sum_{k=1}^{7} 2 \cdot 5^{k-1}$ _____

Infinite Geometric Series

✎ *Determine if each geometric series converges or diverges.*

1) $a_1 = -3, r = 4$

2) $a_1 = 5.5, r = 0.5$

3) $a_1 = -1, r = 3$

4) $a_1 = 3.2, r = 0.2$

5) $a_1 = 5, r = 2$

6) $-1, 3, -9, 27, \ldots$

7) $2, -1, \frac{1}{2}, -\frac{1}{4}, \frac{1}{8}, \ldots$

8) $81 + 27 + 9 + 3 \ldots$

9) $-3 + \frac{12}{5} - \frac{48}{25} + \frac{192}{125} \ldots$

10) $\frac{128}{3,125} - \frac{64}{625} + \frac{32}{125} - \frac{16}{25} \ldots$

✎ *Evaluate each infinite geometric series described.*

11) $a_1 = 3, r = -\frac{1}{5}$

12) $a_1 = 1, r = -3$

13) $a_1 = 1, r = -4$

14) $a_1 = 3, r = \frac{1}{2}$

15) $1 + 0.5 + 0.25 + 0.125 + \cdots$

16) $81 - 27 + 9 - 3 \ldots,$

17) $1 - 0.6 + 0.36 - 0.216 \ldots,$

18) $3 + \frac{9}{4} + \frac{27}{16} + \frac{81}{64} \ldots,$

19) $\sum_{k=1}^{\infty} 4^{k-1}$

20) $\sum_{i=1}^{\infty} (\frac{1}{3})^{i-1}$

21) $\sum_{k=1}^{\infty} (-\frac{1}{3})^{k-1}$

22) $\sum_{n=1}^{\infty} 16(\frac{1}{4})^{n-1}$

Answers of Worksheets – Chapter 15

Arithmetic Sequences

1) $-5, -9, -13$
2) $7, 14, 21$
3) $18, 21, 24$
4) $24, 28, 32$
5) First Five Terms: $24, 26, 28, 30, 32$, Explicit: $a_n = 2n + 22$
6) First Five Terms: $-15, -20, -25, -30, -35$, Explicit: $a_n = -5n - 10$
7) First Five Terms: $18, 28, 38, 48, 58$, Explicit: $a_n = 10n + 8$
8) First Five Terms: $-38, -138, -238, -338, -438$, Explicit: $a_n = -100n + 62$
9) First Five Terms: $-31, -38, -45, -52, -59$, Explicit: $a_n = -7n - 24$
10) First Five Terms: $-39, -31, -23, -15, -7$, Explicit: $a_n = 8n - 47$
11) First Five Terms: $-12.5, -13.6, -14.7, -15.8, -16.9$, Explicit: $a_n = -1.1n - 11.4$
12) First Five Terms: $-21, -51, -81, -111, -141$, Explicit: $a_n = -30n + 9$
13) Next 3 terms: $-46, -48, -50$, Recursive: $a_n = a_{n-1} - 2, a_1 = -2$
14) Next 3 terms: $30.4, 32.2, 34$, Recursive: $a_n = a_{n-1} + 1.8, a_1 = 8.8$
15) Next 3 terms: $28.5, 29.6, 30.7$, Recursive: $a_n = a_{n-1} + 1.1, a_1 = 8.7$
16) Next 3 terms: $-0.8, -0.2, 0.4$, Recursive: $a_n = a_{n-1} + 0.6, a_1 = -13.4$

Geometric Sequences

1) $r = -5$
2) $r = 2$
3) not geometric
4) $r = 5$
5) First Five Terms: $0.8, -4, 20, -100, 500$

   Explicit: $a_n = 0.8 \cdot (-5)^{n-1}$

6) First Five Terms: $1, 2, 4, 8, 16$

   Explicit: $a_n = 2^{n-1}$

7) Common Ratio: $r = 2$

   First Five Terms: $2, 4, 8, 16, 32$

   Explicit: $a_n = 2 \cdot 2^{n-1}$

8) Common Ratio: $r = -3$

   First Five Terms: $-3, 9, -27, 81, -243$

Explicit: $a_n = -3 \cdot (-3)^{n-1}$

9) Common Ratio: $r = 5$

First Five Terms: $2, 10, 50, 250, 1,250$

Explicit: $a_n = 2 \cdot 5^{n-1}$

10) Common Ratio: $r = 3$

First Five Terms: $-3, -9, -27, -81, -243$

Explicit: $a_n = -3 \cdot 3^{n-1}$

11) $a_8 = \dfrac{3}{4}$, Recursive: $a_n = a_{n-1} \cdot \dfrac{-1}{2}, a_1 = -96$

$a_8 = 49,152$, Recursive: $a_n = a_{n-1} \cdot 4, a_1 =$

Comparing Arithmetic and Geometric Sequences

1) Arithmetic
2) Arithmetic
3) Neither
4) Neither
5) Neither
6) Neither
7) Geometric
8) Neither
9) Arithmetic
10) Geometric

11) Arithmetic
12) Neither
13) Arithmetic
14) Geometric
15) Geometric
16) Arithmetic
17) Arithmetic
18) Arithmetic
19) Geometric
20) Arithmetic

21) Neither
22) Arithmetic
23) Geometric
24) Geometric
25) Neither
26) Neither
27) Neither
28) Neither
29) Arithmetic

Finite Geometric

1) 104
2) −122
3) 51
4) 518
5) −124
6) 781
7) 63

8) 52,429
9) −19,682
10) −130,208
11) 13,021
12) −513
13) −21,845
14) −9,842

15) −170
16) 39,364
17) −59048
18) 171
19) 292,968
20) 39,062

Infinite Geometric

1) Diverges

2) Converges

3) Diverges

4) Converges

5) Converges

6) Diverges

7) Converges

8) Converges

9) Converges

10) Diverges

11) $\frac{5}{2}$

12) Infinite

13) Infinite

14) 6

15) 2

16) $\frac{243}{4}$

17) 0.625

18) 12

19) Infinite

20) $\frac{3}{2}$

21) $\frac{3}{4}$

22) $\frac{64}{3}$

"Effortless Math" Publications

Effortless Math authors' team strives to prepare and publish the best quality Mathematics learning resources to make learning Math easier for all. We hope that our publications help you or your student Math in an effective way.

We all in Effortless Math wish you good luck and successful studies!

Effortless Math Authors

www.EffortlessMath.com

... So Much More Online!

✓ FREE Math lessons

✓ More Math learning books!

✓ Mathematics Worksheets

✓ Online Math Tutors

Need a PDF version of this book?

Please visit www.EffortlessMath.com

Made in the USA
San Bernardino,
CA